Cambridge IELTS 3

...mination papers from the
...ersity of Cambridge
...l Examinations Syndicate

CAMBRIDGE UNIVERSITY PRESS
Cambridge, New York, Melbourne, Madrid, Cape Town, Singapore,
São Paulo, Delhi, Dubai, Tokyo

Cambridge University Press
The Edinburgh Building, Cambridge CB2 8RU, UK

www.cambridge.org
Information on this title: www.cambridge.org/9780521013338

First published 2002
10th printing 2009

Printed in the United Kingdom at the University Press, Cambridge

A catalogue record for this publication is available from the British Library

ISBN 978-0-521-01333-8 Student's Book with answers
ISBN 978-0-521-01335-2 Cassette Set
ISBN 978-0-521-01336-9 Audio CD Set
ISBN 978-0-521-01337-6 Self-study Pack

Contents

Acknowledgements

The authors and publishers are grateful to the authors, publishers and others who have given permission for the use of copyright material identified in the text. It has not been possible to identify the sources of all the material used and in such cases the publishers would welcome information from copyright owners. Apologies are expressed for any omissions.

Text p.24 from an extract *'Getting into the* System' in How to Get a PhD 3rd edition by Estelle Phillips and Derek Pugh, published in 1994 by © Open University Press 2000; Text p.38–39 from adapted text *'A Hard earned Pat for a True Digger'* by John Feehan, Volume 20, published in 1994 by © Australian Geographic; Text 43–44 an extract from *'Natural Resource Management – the case of Farm Subsidies'* by Frances Cairncross, Published in 1995 by © *Kogan Page*; Text p.60 an extract from *'Collecting the 20th Century' from the Department of Ethnography* by Frances Carey, published in by The British Museum Press; Text p.84–85 an extract *'Must Megacities mean Megapollution',* from © The Economist Newspaper Limited, London September 1994; Text p.88–89 an extract from *'Nelson's Column, Votes for Women'* by Mary Alexander, *published in 1992 by* © *The Illustrated London News;* Text p.92–92 Reprinted by Permission of *Harvard Business Review,* from '*Management: A Book of Readings*' by *Harold Koontz*, Volume 36, March–April 1958. Copyright © 1958 by the Harvard Business School Publishing Corporation; all rights reserved; Text p.100–101 Enrolment details, conditions and fees, published in 1995 by The Francis King School of English; Text p.106 an extract from *'the University of Waikato Language Institute New Zealand'*, published in 1995 by © Waikato University; Text p.122–123 © Alan Mitchell/Times Newspapers Limited, London 16 October 1995.

The publishers are grateful to the following for permission to include photographs:

Art Directors & **TRIP/R** Nichols for p. 47; Robert Harding Picture Library for p. 58; Tony Waltham for pp. 84, 108(r); Paul Mulcahy for p. 19; Popperfoto for pp. 88, 106; Science Photo Library/Crown Copyright/Health and Safety Laboratory for p. 108(1); John Reader for p. 38; South American Pictures/Marion & Tony Morrison for p. 60.

Picture research by Valerie Mulcahy
Design concept by Peter Ducker MSTD

Cover design by John Dunne

The cassettes and audio CDs which accompany this book were recorded at Studio AVP, London.

Introduction

The International English Language Testing System (IELTS) is widely recognised as a reliable means of assessing whether candidates are ready to study or train in the medium of English. IELTS is owned by three partners, the University of Cambridge Local Examinations Syndicate, the British Council and IDP Education Australia (through its subsidiary company IELTS Australia Pty Limited). The main purpose of this book of Practice Tests is to give future IELTS candidates an idea of whether their English is at the required level. Further information on IELTS can be found in the IELTS Handbook available free of charge from IELTS centres.

WHAT IS THE TEST FORMAT?

IELTS consists of six modules. All candidates take the same Listening and Speaking modules. There is a choice of Reading and Writing modules according to whether a candidate is taking the Academic or General Training version of the test.

Academic	General Training
For candidates taking the test for entry to undergraduate or postgraduate studies or for professional reasons	For candidates taking the test for entry to vocational or training programmes not at degree level, for admission to secondary schools and for immigration purposes

The test modules are taken in the following order:

Listening
4 sections, 40 items
30 minutes

Academic Reading		General Training Reading
3 sections, 40 items	OR	3 sections, 40 items
60 minutes		60 minutes

Academic Writing		General Training Writing
2 tasks	OR	2 tasks
60 minutes		60 minutes

Speaking
11 to 14 minutes

Total test time
2 hours 44 minutes

Listening

This is in four sections, each with 10 questions. The first two sections are concerned with social needs. There is a conversation between two speakers and then a monologue. The final two sections are concerned with situations related to educational or training contexts. There is a conversation between up to four people and then a monologue.

A variety of question types is used, including: multiple choice, short-answer questions, sentence completion, notes/chart/table completion, labelling a diagram, classification, matching.

Candidates hear the recording once only and answer the questions as they listen. Ten minutes are allowed at the end to transfer answers to the answer sheet.

Academic Reading

There are three reading passages, of increasing difficulty, on topics of general interest and candidates have to answer 40 questions. The passages are taken from magazines, journals, books and newspapers. At least one text contains detailed logical argument.

A variety of question types is used, including: multiple choice, short-answer questions, sentence completion, notes/chart/table completion, labelling a diagram, classification, matching lists/phrases, choosing suitable paragraph headings from a list, identification of writer's views/attitudes – yes, no, not given, or true, false, not given.

General Training Reading

Candidates have to answer 40 questions. There are three sections of increasing difficulty, containing texts taken from notices, advertisements, leaflets, newspapers, instruction manuals, books and magazines. The first section contains texts relevant to basic linguistic survival in English, with tasks mainly concerned with providing factual information. The second section focuses on the training context and involves texts of more complex language. The third section involves reading more extended texts, with a more complex structure, but with the emphasis on descriptive and instructive rather than argumentative texts.

A variety of question types is used, including: multiple choice, short-answer questions, sentence completion, notes/chart/table completion, labelling a diagram, classification, matching lists/phrases, choosing suitable paragraph headings from a list, identification of writer's views/attitudes – yes, no, not given, or true, false, not given.

Academic Writing

There are two tasks and it is suggested that candidates spend about 20 minutes on Task 1, which requires them to write at least 150 words, and 40 minutes on Task 2 – 250 words. The assessment of Task 2 carries more weight in marking than Task 1.

In Task 1 candidates are asked to look at a diagram or table and to present the information in their own words. They are assessed on their ability to organise, present and possibly compare data, describe the stages of a process, describe an object or event, explain how something works.

In Task 2 candidates are presented with a point of view, argument or problem. They are assessed on their ability to present a solution to the problem, present and justify an opinion, compare and contrast evidence and opinions, evaluate and challenge ideas, evidence or arguments.

Candidates are also judged on their ability to write in an appropriate style.

General Training Writing

There are two tasks and it is suggested that candidates spend about 20 minutes on Task 1, which requires them to write at least 150 words, and 40 minutes on Task 2 – 250 words. The assessment of Task 2 carries more weight in marking than Task 1.

In Task 1 candidates are asked to respond to a given problem with a letter requesting information or explaining a situation. They are assessed on their ability to engage in personal correspondence, elicit and provide general factual information, express needs, wants, likes and dislikes, express opinions, complaints, etc.

In Task 2 candidates are presented with a point of view, argument or problem. They are assessed on their ability to provide general factual information, outline a problem and present a solution, present and justify an opinion, evaluate and challenge ideas, evidence or arguments.

Candidates are also judged on their ability to write in an appropriate style.

Speaking

The Speaking module takes between 11 and 14 minutes. It consists of an oral interview between the candidate and an examiner.

There are three main parts:

Part 1
The candidate and the examiner introduce themselves and then the candidate answers general questions about themselves, their home/family, their job/studies, their interests and a wide range of similar familiar topic areas. This part lasts between four and five minutes.

Part 2
The candidate is given a task card with prompts and is asked to talk on a particular topic. The candidate has one minute to prepare and they can make some notes if they wish, before speaking for between one and two minutes. The examiner then asks one or two rounding-off questions.

Part 3
The examiner and the candidate engage in a discussion of more abstract issues and concepts, which are thematically linked to the topic prompt in Part 2. The discussion lasts between four and five minutes.

The Speaking module assesses whether candidates can communicate effectively in English. The assessment takes into account Fluency and Coherence, Lexical Resource, Grammatical Range and Accuracy, and Pronunciation.

HOW IS IELTS SCORED?

IELTS results are reported on a nine-band scale. In addition to the score for overall language ability IELTS provides a score, in the form of a profile, for each of the four skills (Listening, Reading, Writing and Speaking). These scores are also reported on a nine-band scale. All scores are recorded on the Test Report Form along with details of the candidate's nationality, first language and date of birth. Each Overall Band Score corresponds to a descriptive statement which gives a summary of the English language ability of a candidate classified at that level. The nine bands and their descriptive statements are as follows:

9 Expert User – *Has fully operational command of the language: appropriate, accurate and fluent with complete understanding.*

8 Very Good User – *Has fully operational command of the language with only occasional unsystematic inaccuracies and inappropriacies. Misunderstandings may occur in unfamiliar situations. Handles complex detailed argumentation well.*

7 Good User – *Has operational command of the language, though occasional inaccuracies, inappropriacies and misunderstandings in some situations. Generally handles complex language well and understands detailed reasoning.*

6 Competent User – *Has generally effective command of the language despite some inaccuracies, inappropriacies and misunderstandings. Can use and understand fairly complex language, particularly in familiar situations.*

5 Modest User – *Has partial command of the language, coping with overall meaning in most situations, though is likely to make many mistakes. Should be able to handle basic communication in own field.*

4 Limited User – *Basic competence is limited to familiar situations. Has frequent problems in understanding and expression. Is not able to use complex language.*

3 Extremely Limited User – *Conveys and understands only general meaning in very familiar situations. Frequent breakdowns in communication occur.*

2 Intermittent User – *No real communication is possible except for the most basic information using isolated words or short formulae in familiar situations and to meet immediate needs. Has great difficulty understanding spoken and written English.*

1 Non User – *Essentially has no ability to use the language beyond possibly a few isolated words.*

0 Did not attempt the test. – *No assessable information.*

Most universities and colleges in the United Kingdom, Australia, New Zealand and Canada accept an IELTS Overall Band Score of 6.0 or 6.5 for entry to academic programmes. IELTS scores are increasingly being recognised by universities in the USA.

MARKING THE PRACTICE TESTS

Listening and Reading

The Answer key is on pages 149–158.

Each item in the Listening and Reading tests is worth one mark. There are no half marks. Put a tick (✓) next to each correct answer and a cross (✗) next to each wrong one. Each tick will equal one mark.

Single letter/number answers
- For questions where the answer is a single letter or number, you should write **only** one answer. If you have written more than one, the answer must be marked wrong.

Longer answers
- Only the answers given in the Answer key are correct. If you write something different to the answer given in the key, it should be marked wrong.
- Answers may be written in upper or lower case.
- Sometimes part of the correct answer is given in brackets. Words in brackets are optional – they are correct, but not necessary.
- Alternative words or phrases within an answer are indicated by a single slash (/).
- Sometimes there are alternative correct answers to a question. In these cases the possible answers are separated by a double slash (//). If you have written any one of these possible answers, your answer is correct.
- You will find additional notes about individual questions in the Answer key.

Spelling
- All answers require correct spelling unless alternative spellings are stated in the Answer key. If a word is spelt differently from the Answer key, it should be marked wrong.
- Both US and UK spelling are acceptable.

Writing

Obviously it is not possible for you to give yourself a mark for the Writing tasks. For Tests 2 and 3 and GT Test A we have provided *model answers* (written by an examiner) at the back of the book. It is important to note that these show just one way of completing the task, out of many possible approaches. For Tests 1 and 4 and GT Test B we have provided *sample answers* (written by candidates), showing their score and the examiner's comments. We hope that both of these will give you an insight into what is required for the Writing module.

HOW SHOULD YOU INTERPRET YOUR SCORES?

In the Answer key at the end of each set of Listening and Reading answers you will find a chart which will help you assess if, on the basis of your practice test results, you are ready to take the IELTS exam.

In interpreting your score, there are a number of points you should bear in mind.

Your performance in the real IELTS test will be reported in two ways: there will be a Band Score from 1 to 9 for each of the modules and an Overall Band Score from 1 to 9, which is the average of your scores in the four modules.

However, institutions considering your application are advised to look at both the Overall Band and the Bands for each module. They do this in order to see if you have the language skills needed for a particular course of study. For example, if your course has a lot of reading and writing, but no lectures, listening comprehension might be less important and a score of 5 in Listening might be acceptable if the Overall Band Score was 7. However, for a course where there are lots of lectures and spoken instructions, a score of 5 in Listening might be unacceptable even though the Overall Band Score was 7.

Once you have marked your papers you should have some idea of whether your Listening and Reading skills are good enough for you to try the real IELTS test. If you did well enough in one module but not in others, you will have to decide for yourself whether you are ready to take the proper test yet.

The Practice Tests have been checked so that they are about the same level of difficulty as the real IELTS test. However, we cannot guarantee that your score in the Practice Test papers will be reflected in the real IELTS test. The Practice Tests can only give you an idea of your possible future performance and it is ultimately up to you to make decisions based on your score.

Different institutions accept different IELTS scores for different types of courses. We have based our recommendations on the average scores which the majority of institutions accept. The institution to which you are applying may, of course, require a higher or lower score than most other institutions.

Sample answers or model answers are provided for the Writing tasks. The sample answers were written by IELTS candidates; each answer has been given a band score and the candidate's performance is described. Please note that the examiner's guidelines for marking the Writing scripts are very detailed. There are many different ways a candidate may achieve a particular band score. The model answers were written by an examiner as examples of very good answers, but it is important to understand that they are just one example out of many possible approaches.

Further information

For more information about IELTS or any other UCLES examination write to:

EFL Division
UCLES
1 Hills Road
Cambridge
CB1 2EU
England

Telephone: +44 1223 553311
Fax: +44 1223 460278
e-mail: efl@ucles.org.uk
http://www.cambridge-efl.org.uk

Test 1

SECTION 1   Questions 1–10

Complete the notes below.

Example	Answer
Name of agent:	**Flagstone**

Areas dealt with: **1** ....

north suburbs

Rent: from **2** £ .... to £ .... a month

Depends on: the area
availability of **3** ....
garage

Properties available: West Park Road
rent **4** £ .... a month
including **5** ....

Tithe Road
rent £380 a month
including **6** .... rental

Viewing arrangements: meet at office on **7** .... at 5.00 pm

Need: letter from bank
reference from **8** ....

Must: give **9** .... notice of moving in
give deposit of **10** ....
pay for contract

SECTION 2   *Questions 11–20*

Questions 11 and 12

*Write **NO MORE THAN THREE WORDS** for each answer.*

11   Who is Mrs Sutton worried about?

....

12   What is the name for a group of family doctors working in the same building together?

....

Questions 13–17

Complete the table below.

*Write **NO MORE THAN THREE WORDS OR A NUMBER** for each answer.*

Name of Health Centre	Number of doctors	Other information	Information about doctors
Dean End	**13**	Appointment system **15** .... than South Hay	Dr Jones is good with **16** .... patients. Dr Shaw is good with small children.
South Hay	**14**	Building less modern than Dean End	Dr Williams helps people with **17** ....

Questions 18–20

Question 18

Write **NO MORE THAN TWO WORDS OR A NUMBER**.

Doctors start seeing patients at the Health Centre from .... o'clock.

Question 19

Choose **TWO** *letters A–E.*

Which **TWO** groups of patients receive free medication?

A   people over 17 years old
B   unemployed people
C   non-UK residents
D   people over 60 years old
E   pregnant women

Question 20

Write **NO MORE THAN TWO WORDS OR A NUMBER**.

The charge for one item of medication is about £ ....

SECTION 3   *Questions 21–30*

Complete the notes below.

Write **NUMBERS AND/OR NO MORE THAN THREE WORDS** *for each answer.*

NOTES ON APPLICATION	
Name:	Jonathan Briggs
Degree:	Economics and 21 ....
Teaching experience:	Volunteer Teacher
Location:	22 ....
Dates:	23 ....
Volunteer Organisation:	24 ....
Type of school:	25 ....
Subjects taught:	26 .... Forms 1, 2 and 3
	• English Form 27 ....
	• Agricultural Science Form 6
Other responsibilities:	ran school farm

NOTES (continued)

Reasons for wanting to leave in first year:	• 28 .... • few teaching resources
Reasons for wanting to extend tour:	• success of cattle breeding project • obtained funds for farm buildings
Reasons for wanting to train to teach Geography:	• It is his 29 .... • It has many 30 ....

SECTION 4   *Questions 31–40*

Questions 31–36

Choose the correct letters A–C.

31   Which column of the bar chart represents the figures quoted?

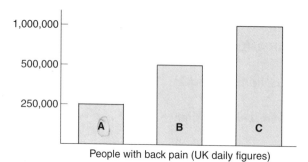

People with back pain (UK daily figures)

32   According to the speaker, the main cause of back pain in women is

    A   pregnancy.
    B   osteoporosis.
    C   lack of exercise.

33   As treatment for back pain the Clinic mainly recommends

    A   pain killers.
    B   relaxation therapy.
    C   exercise routines.

34   The back is different from other parts of the body because

    A   it is usually better at self-repair.
    B   a back injury is usually more painful.
    C   its response to injury often results in more damage.

35   Bed rest is advised

    A   for a maximum of two days.
    B   for extreme pain only.
    C   for pain lasting more than two days.

36   Being overweight

    A   is a major source of back pain.
    B   worsens existing back pain.
    C   reduces the effectiveness of exercise.

Questions 37–40

Choose the correct letters A–C.

	Strongly recommended A	Recommended in certain circumstances B	Not recommended C
Example Diet if overweight	*Answer* (A)	B	C
37 Buy special orthopaedic chairs	A	B	C
Example Buy orthopaedic mattresses	A	*Answer* (B)	C
38 Buy shock-absorbing inserts	A	B	C
39 Wear flat shoes	A	B	C
40 Buy TENS machine	A	B	C

READING

READING PASSAGE 1

*You should spend about 20 minutes on **Questions 1–14** which are based on Reading Passage 1 on the following pages.*

Questions 1–4

Reading Passage 1 has six paragraphs **A–F**.
*Choose the most suitable headings for paragraphs **B–E** from the list of headings below.*
*Write the appropriate numbers **i–ix** in boxes 1–4 on your answer sheet.*

List of Headings

i   How the reaction principle works
ii   The impact of the reaction principle
iii   Writers' theories of the reaction principle
iv   Undeveloped for centuries
v   The first rockets
vi   The first use of steam
vii   Rockets for military use
viii   Developments of fire
ix   What's next?

Example	*Answer*
Paragraph **A**	**ii**

1   Paragraph **B**

2   Paragraph **C**

3   Paragraph **D**

4   Paragraph **E**

Example	*Answer*
Paragraph **F**	**ix**

THE ROCKET – FROM EAST TO WEST

A The concept of the rocket, or rather the mechanism behind the idea of propelling an object into the air, has been around for well over two thousand years. However, it wasn't until the discovery of the reaction principle, which was the key to space travel and so represents one of the great milestones in the history of scientific thought, that rocket technology was able to develop. Not only did it solve a problem that had intrigued man for ages, but, more importantly, it literally opened the door to exploration of the universe.

B An intellectual breakthrough, brilliant though it may be, does not automatically ensure that the transition is made from theory to practice. Despite the fact that rockets had been used sporadically for several hundred years, they remained a relatively minor artefact of civilisation until the twentieth century. Prodigious efforts, accelerated during two world wars, were required before the technology of primitive rocketry could be translated into the reality of sophisticated astronauts. It is strange that the rocket was generally ignored by writers of fiction to transport their heroes to mysterious realms beyond the Earth, even though it had been commonly used in fireworks displays in China since the thirteenth century. The reason is that nobody associated the reaction principle with the idea of travelling through space to a neighbouring world.

C A simple analogy can help us to understand how a rocket operates. It is much like a machine gun mounted on the rear of a boat. In reaction to the backward discharge of bullets, the gun, and hence the boat, move forwards. A rocket motor's 'bullets' are minute, high-speed particles produced by burning propellants in a suitable chamber. The reaction to the ejection of these small particles causes the rocket to move forwards. There is evidence that the reaction principle was applied practically well before the rocket was invented. In his *Noctes Atticae* or *Greek Nights*, Aulus Gellius describes 'the pigeon of Archytas', an invention dating back to about 360 BC. Cylindrical in shape, made of wood, and hanging from string, it was moved to and fro by steam blowing out from small exhaust ports at either end. The reaction to the discharging steam provided the bird with motive power.

D The invention of rockets is linked inextricably with the invention of 'black powder'. Most historians of technology credit the Chinese with its discovery. They base their belief on studies of Chinese writings or on the notebooks of early Europeans who settled in or made long visits to China to study its history and civilisation. It is probable that, some time in the tenth century, black powder was first compounded from its basic ingredients of saltpetre, charcoal and sulphur. But this does not mean that it was immediately used to propel rockets. By the thirteenth century, powder-propelled fire arrows had become rather common. The Chinese relied on this type of technological development to produce incendiary projectiles of many sorts, explosive grenades and possibly cannons to repel their enemies. One such weapon was the 'basket of fire' or, as directly translated from Chinese, the 'arrows like flying leopards'. The 0.7 metre-long arrows, each with a long tube of gunpowder attached near the point of each arrow, could be fired from a long, octagonal-shaped basket at the same time and had a range of 400 paces. Another weapon was the 'arrow as a flying sabre', which could be fired from crossbows. The rocket, placed in a similar position to other rocket-propelled arrows, was designed to increase the range. A small iron weight was attached to the 1.5m bamboo shaft, just below the feathers, to increase the arrow's stability by moving the centre of gravity to a position below the rocket. At a similar time, the Arabs had developed the 'egg which moves and burns'. This 'egg' was apparently full of gunpowder and stabilised by a 1.5m tail. It was fired using two rockets attached to either side of this tail.

E It was not until the eighteenth century that Europe became seriously interested in the possibilities of using the rocket itself as a weapon of war and not just to propel other weapons. Prior to this, rockets were used only in pyrotechnic displays. The incentive for the more aggressive use of rockets came not from within the European continent but from far-away India, whose leaders had built up a corps of rocketeers and used rockets successfully against the British in the late eighteenth century. The Indian rockets used against the British were described by a British Captain serving in India as 'an iron envelope about 200 millimetres long and 40 millimetres in diameter with sharp points at the top and a 3m-long bamboo guiding stick'. In the early nineteenth century the British began to experiment with incendiary barrage rockets. The British rocket differed from the Indian version in that it was completely encased in a stout, iron cylinder, terminating in a conical head, measuring one metre in diameter and having a stick almost five metres long and constructed in such a way that it could be firmly attached to the body of the rocket. The Americans developed a rocket, complete with its own launcher, to use against the Mexicans in the mid-nineteenth century. A long cylindrical tube was propped up by two sticks and fastened to the top of the launcher, thereby allowing the rockets to be inserted and lit from the other end. However, the results were sometimes not that impressive as the behaviour of the rockets in flight was less than predictable.

F Since then, there have been huge developments in rocket technology, often with devastating results in the forum of war. Nevertheless, the modern day space programs owe their success to the humble beginnings of those in previous centuries who developed the foundations of the reaction principle. Who knows what it will be like in the future?

Questions 5 and 6

*Choose the appropriate letters **A–D** and write them in boxes 5 and 6 on your answer sheet.*

5   The greatest outcome of the discovery of the reaction principle was that

    A   rockets could be propelled into the air.
    B   space travel became a reality.
    C   a major problem had been solved.
    D   bigger rockets were able to be built.

6   According to the text, the greatest progress in rocket technology was made

    A   from the tenth to the thirteenth centuries.
    B   from the seventeenth to the nineteenth centuries.
    C   from the early nineteenth to the late nineteenth century.
    D   from the late nineteenth century to the present day.

Questions 7–10

*From the information in the text, indicate who **FIRST** invented or used the items in the list below.*
*Write the appropriate letters **A–E** in boxes 7–10 on your answer sheet.*
NB You may use any letter more than once.

Example	Answer
rockets for displays	**A**

7   black powder

8   rocket-propelled arrows for fighting

9   rockets as war weapons

10   the rocket launcher

FIRST invented or used by
A   the Chinese
B   the Indians
C   the British
D   the Arabs
E   the Americans

Questions 11–14

*Look at the drawings of different projectiles below, **A–H**, and the names of types of projectiles given in the passage, **Questions 11–14**. Match each name with one drawing.*

*Write the appropriate letters **A–H** in boxes 11–14 on your answer sheet.*

Example	*Answer*
The Greek 'pigeon of Archytas'	**C**

11 The Chinese 'basket of fire'

12 The Arab 'egg which moves and burns'

13 The Indian rocket

14 The British barrage rocket

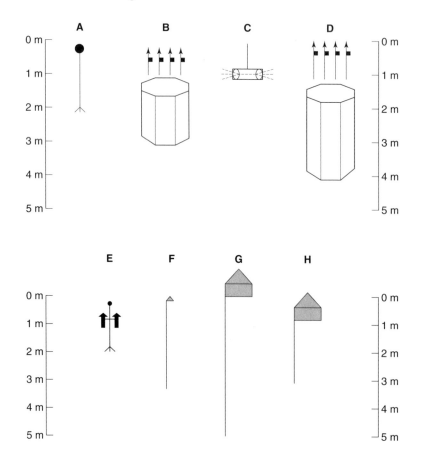

READING PASSAGE 2

*You should spend about 20 minutes on **Questions 15–28** which are based on Reading Passage 2 below.*

The Risks of Cigarette Smoke

Discovered in the early 1800s and named nicotianine, the oily essence now called nicotine is the main active ingredient of tobacco. Nicotine, however, is only a small component of cigarette smoke, which contains more than 4,700 chemical compounds, including 43 cancer-causing substances. In recent times, scientific research has been providing evidence that years of cigarette smoking vastly increases the risk of developing fatal medical conditions.

In addition to being responsible for more than 85 per cent of lung cancers, smoking is associated with cancers of, amongst others, the mouth, stomach and kidneys, and is thought to cause about 14 per cent of leukemia and cervical cancers. In 1990, smoking caused more than 84,000 deaths, mainly resulting from such problems as pneumonia, bronchitis and influenza. Smoking, it is believed, is responsible for 30 per cent of all deaths from cancer and clearly represents the most important preventable cause of cancer in countries like the United States today.

Passive smoking, the breathing in of the side-stream smoke from the burning of tobacco between puffs or of the smoke exhaled by a smoker, also causes a serious health risk. A report published in 1992 by the US Environmental Protection Agency (EPA) emphasized the health dangers, especially from side-stream smoke. This type of smoke contains more, smaller particles and is therefore more likely to be deposited deep in the lungs. On the basis of this report, the EPA has classified environmental tobacco smoke in the highest risk category for causing cancer.

As an illustration of the health risks, in the case of a married couple where one partner is a smoker and one a non-smoker, the latter is believed to have a 30 per cent higher risk of death from heart disease because of passive smoking. The risk of lung cancer also increases over the years of exposure and the figure jumps to 80 per cent if the spouse has been smoking four packs a day for 20 years. It has been calculated that 17 per cent of cases of lung cancer can be attributed to high levels of exposure to second-hand tobacco smoke during childhood and adolescence.

A more recent study by researchers at the University of California at San Francisco (UCSF) has shown that second-hand cigarette smoke does more harm to non-smokers than to smokers. Leaving aside the philosophical question of whether anyone should have to breathe someone else's cigarette smoke, the report suggests that the smoke experienced by many people in their daily lives is enough to produce substantial adverse effects on a person's heart and lungs.

The report, published in the Journal of the American Medical Association (AMA), was based on the researchers' own earlier research but also includes a review of studies over the past few years. The American Medical Association represents about half of all US doctors and is a strong opponent of smoking. The study suggests that people who smoke cigarettes are continually damaging their cardiovascular system, which adapts in order to compensate for the effects of smoking. It further states that people who do not smoke do not have the benefit of their system adapting to the smoke inhalation. Consequently, the effects of passive smoking are far greater on non-smokers than on smokers.

This report emphasizes that cancer is not caused by a single element in cigarette smoke; harmful effects to health are caused by many components. Carbon monoxide, for example, competes with oxygen in red blood cells and interferes with the blood's ability to deliver life-giving oxygen to the heart. Nicotine and other toxins in cigarette smoke activate small blood cells called platelets, which increases the likelihood of blood clots, thereby affecting blood circulation throughout the body.

The researchers criticize the practice of some scientific consultants who work with the tobacco industry for assuming that cigarette smoke has the same impact on smokers as it does on non-smokers. They argue that those scientists are underestimating the damage done by passive smoking and, in support of their recent findings, cite some previous research which points to passive smoking as the cause for between 30,000 and 60,000 deaths from heart attacks each year in the United States. This means that passive smoking is the third most preventable cause of death after active smoking and alcohol-related diseases.

The study argues that the type of action needed against passive smoking should be similar to that being taken against illegal drugs and AIDS (SIDA). The UCSF researchers maintain that the simplest and most cost-effective action is to establish smoke-free work places, schools and public places.

Questions 15–17

*Choose the appropriate letters **A–D** and write them in boxes 15–17 on your answer sheet.*

15   According to information in the text, leukaemia and pneumonia

       A   are responsible for 84,000 deaths each year.
       B   are strongly linked to cigarette smoking.
       C   are strongly linked to lung cancer.
       D   result in 30 per cent of deaths per year.

16   According to information in the text, intake of carbon monoxide

       A   inhibits the flow of oxygen to the heart.
       B   increases absorption of other smoke particles.
       C   inhibits red blood cell formation.
       D   promotes nicotine absorption.

17   According to information in the text, intake of nicotine encourages

       A   blood circulation through the body.
       B   activity of other toxins in the blood.
       C   formation of blood clots.
       D   an increase of platelets in the blood.

Questions 18–21

Do the following statements reflect the claims of the writer in Reading Passage 2?

In boxes 18–21 on your answer sheet write

     YES   *if the statement reflects the claims of the writer*
     NO   *if the statement contradicts the claims of the writer*
     NOT GIVEN   *if it is impossible to say what the writer thinks about this*

18   Thirty per cent of deaths in the United States are caused by smoking-related diseases.

19   If one partner in a marriage smokes, the other is likely to take up smoking.

20   Teenagers whose parents smoke are at risk of getting lung cancer at some time during their lives.

21   Opponents of smoking financed the UCSF study.

Questions 22–24

*Choose **ONE** phrase from the list of phrases A–J below to complete each of the following sentences (Questions 22–24).*

Write the appropriate letters in boxes 22–24 on your answer sheet.

22   Passive smoking ... G

23   Compared with a non-smoker, a smoker ...

24   The American Medical Association ...

A	includes reviews of studies in its reports.
B	argues for stronger action against smoking in public places.
C	is one of the two most preventable causes of death.
D	is more likely to be at risk from passive smoking diseases.
E	is more harmful to non-smokers than to smokers.
F	is less likely to be at risk of contracting lung cancer.
G	is more likely to be at risk of contracting various cancers.
H	opposes smoking and publishes research on the subject.
I	is just as harmful to smokers as it is to non-smokers.
J	reduces the quantity of blood flowing around the body.

Questions 25–28

Classify the following statements as being

> **A**   *a finding of the UCSF study*
> **B**   *an opinion of the UCSF study*
> **C**   *a finding of the EPA report*
> **D**   *an assumption of consultants to the tobacco industry*

Write the appropriate letters A–D in boxes 25–28 on your answer sheet.

NB   You may use any letter more than once.

25   Smokers' cardiovascular systems adapt to the intake of environmental smoke.

26   There is a philosophical question as to whether people should have to inhale others' smoke.

27   Smoke-free public places offer the best solution.

28   The intake of side-stream smoke is more harmful than smoke exhaled by a smoker.

READING PASSAGE 3

*You should spend about 20 minutes on **Questions 29–40** which are based on Reading Passage 3 on the following pages.*

Questions 29–33

Reading Passage 3 has seven paragraphs **A–G**.

*Choose the most suitable headings for paragraphs **C–G** from the list of headings below.*

*Write the appropriate numbers **i–x** in boxes 29–33 on your answer sheet.*

List of Headings
i   The Crick and Watson approach to research
ii   Antidotes to bacterial infection
iii   The testing of hypotheses
iv   Explaining the inductive method
v   Anticipating results before data is collected
vi   How research is done and how it is reported
vii   The role of hypotheses in scientific research
viii   Deducing the consequences of hypotheses
ix   Karl Popper's claim that the scientific method is hypothetico-deductive
x   The unbiased researcher

Example	*Answer*
Paragraph **A**	**ix**

29   Paragraph **C**

30   Paragraph **D**

31   Paragraph **E**

32   Paragraph **F**

33   Paragraph **G**

THE SCIENTIFIC METHOD

A 'Hypotheses,' said Medawar in 1964, 'are imaginative and inspirational in character'; they are 'adventures of the mind'. He was arguing in favour of the position taken by Karl Popper in *The Logic of Scientific Discovery* (1972, 3rd edition) that the nature of scientific method is hypothetico-deductive and not, as is generally believed, inductive.

B It is essential that you, as an intending researcher, understand the difference between these two interpretations of the research process so that you do not become discouraged or begin to suffer from a feeling of 'cheating' or not going about it the right way.

C The myth of scientific method is that it is inductive: that the formulation of scientific theory starts with the basic, raw evidence of the senses – simple, unbiased, unprejudiced observation. Out of these sensory data – commonly referred to as 'facts' – generalisations will form. The myth is that from a disorderly array of factual information an orderly, relevant theory will somehow emerge. However, the starting point of induction is an impossible one.

D There is no such thing as an unbiased observation. Every act of observation we make is a function of what we have seen or otherwise experienced in the past. All scientific work of an experimental or exploratory nature starts with some expectation about the outcome. This expectation is a hypothesis. Hypotheses provide the initiative and incentive for the inquiry and influence the method. It is in the light of an expectation that some observations are held to be relevant and some irrelevant, that one methodology is chosen and others discarded, that some experiments are conducted and others are not. Where is your naive, pure and objective researcher now?

E Hypotheses arise by guesswork, or by inspiration, but having been formulated they can and must be tested rigorously, using the appropriate methodology. If the predictions you make as a result of deducing certain consequences from your hypothesis are not shown to be correct then you discard or modify your hypothesis. If the predictions turn out to be correct then your hypothesis has been supported and may be retained until such time as some further test shows it not to be correct. Once you have arrived at your hypothesis, which is a product of your imagination, you then proceed to a strictly logical and rigorous process, based upon deductive argument – hence the term 'hypothetico-deductive'.

F   So don't worry if you have some idea of what your results will tell you before you even begin to collect data; there are no scientists in existence who really wait until they have all the evidence in front of them before they try to work out what it might possibly mean. The closest we ever get to this situation is when something happens by accident; but even then the researcher has to formulate a hypothesis to be tested before being sure that, for example, a mould might prove to be a successful antidote to bacterial infection.

G   The myth of scientific method is not only that it is inductive (which we have seen is incorrect) but also that the hypothetico-deductive method proceeds in a step-by-step, inevitable fashion. The hypothetico-deductive method describes the *logical* approach to much research work, but it does not describe the *psychological* behaviour that brings it about. This is much more holistic – involving guesses, reworkings, corrections, blind alleys and above all inspiration, in the deductive as well as the hypothetic component – than is immediately apparent from reading the final thesis or published papers. These have been, quite properly, organised into a more serial, logical order so that the worth of the *output* may be evaluated independently of the behavioural processes by which it was obtained. It is the difference, for example between the academic papers with which Crick and Watson demonstrated the structure of the DNA molecule and the fascinating book *The Double Helix* in which Watson (1968) described how they did it. From this point of view, 'scientific method' may more usefully be thought of as a way of *writing up* research rather than as a way of carrying it out.

Questions 34 and 35

In which **TWO** paragraphs in Reading Passage 3 does the writer give advice **directly** to the reader?

*Write the **TWO** appropriate letters (A–G) in boxes 34 and 35 on your answer sheet.*

Questions 36–39

Do the following statements reflect the opinions of the writer in Reading Passage 3?

In boxes 36–39 on your answer sheet write

> **YES**   *if the statement reflects the opinion of the writer*
> **NO**   *if the statement contradicts the opinion of the writer*
> **NOT GIVEN** *if it is impossible to say what the writer thinks about this*

36   Popper says that the scientific method is hypothetico-deductive.

37   If a prediction based on a hypothesis is fulfilled, then the hypothesis is confirmed as true.

38   Many people carry out research in a mistaken way.

39   The 'scientific method' is more a way of describing research than a way of doing it.

Question 40

Choose the appropriate letter A–D and write it in box 40 on your answer sheet.

Which of the following statements best describes the writer's main purpose in Reading Passage 3?

A   to advise Ph.D students not to cheat while carrying out research
B   to encourage Ph.D students to work by guesswork and inspiration
C   to explain to Ph.D students the logic which the scientific research paper follows
D   to help Ph.D students by explaining different conceptions of the research process

WRITING

WRITING TASK 1

You should spend about 20 minutes on this task.

> *The charts below show the number of Japanese tourists travelling abroad between 1985 and 1995 and Australia's share of the Japanese tourist market.*
>
> *Write a report for a university lecturer describing the information shown below.*

You should write at least 150 words.

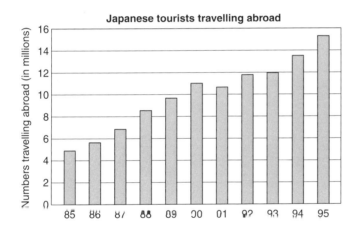

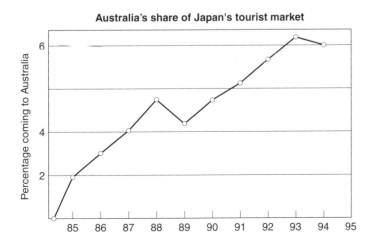

WRITING TASK 2

You should spend about 40 minutes on this task.

Present a written argument or case to an educated reader with no specialist knowledge of the following topic.

> *Popular events like the football World Cup and other international sporting occasions are essential in easing international tensions and releasing patriotic emotions in a safe way.*
>
> *To what extent do you agree or disagree with this opinion?*

You should use your own ideas, knowledge and experience and support your arguments with examples and relevant evidence.

You should write at least 250 words.

SPEAKING

PART 1

The examiner asks the candidate about him/herself, his/her home, work or studies and other familiar topics.

EXAMPLE

Family

- Do you have a large family or a small family?
- Can you tell me something about them?
- How much time do you manage to spend with members of your family?
- What sorts of things do you like to do together?
- Did/Do you get on well with your family? [Why?]

PART 2

> **Describe a teacher who has influenced you in your education.**
> **You should say:**
> > **where you met them**
> > **what subject they taught**
> > **what was special about them**
> **and explain why this person influenced you so much.**

You will have to talk about the topic for 1 to 2 minutes. You have one minute to think about what you're going to say. You can make some notes to help you if you wish.

PART 3

Discussion topics:

Developments in education

Example questions:
How has education changed in your country in the last 10 years?
What changes do you foresee in the next 50 years?

A national education system

Example questions:
How do the expectations of today's school leavers compare with those of the previous generation?
What role do you think extracurricular activities play in education?

Different styles/methods of teaching and learning

Example questions:
What method of learning works best for you?
How beneficial do you think it is to group students according to their level of ability?

Test 2

SECTION 1   Questions 1–10

Questions 1–5

Complete the table below.

Write **NO MORE THAN THREE WORDS OR A NUMBER** *for each answer.*

Programme of Activities for First Day		
Time	**Place**	**Event**
Example **10.00**	**1**	Meet the Principal and staff
10.15		Talk by **2** ....
10.45		Talk by **3** ....
4	Classroom 5	**5** .... test

Questions 6–10

Label the rooms on the map below.

Choose your answers from the box below and write them next to questions 6–10.

CL	Computer Laboratory
DO	Director's Office
L	Library
MH	Main Hall
S	Storeroom
SAR	Self Access Room
SCR	Student Common Room
SR	Staff Room

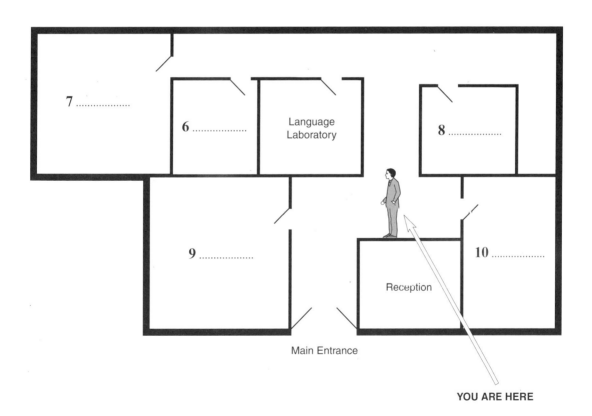

SECTION 2   *Questions 11–20*

Questions 11–15

Complete the table below.

Write **NO MORE THAN THREE WORDS** *for each answer.*

TYPE OF HELP	EXAMPLES
FINANCIAL	• grants • **11** ....
12	• childcare • nurseries
ACADEMIC	• **13** .... • using the library
14	• individual interests • **15** ....

Questions 16–20

Complete the notes below.

*Write **NUMBERS OR NO MORE THAN THREE WORDS** for each answer.*

HELPLINE DETAILS

Officer	Jackie **16** ....
Address	Student Welfare Office
	13 Marshall Road
Telephone number	**17** ....
Opening hours	9.30am – 6pm (weekdays)
	18 .... (Saturdays)
	Ring or visit office for **19** ....
	N.B. At peak times there may be a
	20 ....

SECTION 3   *Questions 21–30*

Questions 21–24

Choose the correct letters A–C.

21   At the start of the tutorial, the tutor emphasises the importance of

    A   interviews.
    B   staff selection.
    C   question techniques.

22   An example of a person who doesn't 'fit in' is someone who

    A   is over-qualified for the job.
    B   lacks experience of the tasks set.
    C   disagrees with the rest of the group.

23   An important part of teamwork is having trust in your

    A   colleagues' ability.
    B   employer's directions.
    C   company training.

24   The tutor says that finding out personal information is

    A   a skill that needs practice.
    B   avoided by many interviewers.
    C   already a part of job interviews.

Questions 25–29

Complete the notes below.

Write **NO MORE THAN THREE WORDS** *for each answer.*

Personality Questionnaires

• completed during 25 ....

• used in the past by the 26 ....

  and the 27 ....

• nowadays used by 28 .... of large

  employers

• questions about things like: working under pressure or

  keeping deadlines

• written by 29 .... who say

  candidates tend to be truthful

Question 30

Choose the correct letter A–C.

What is the tutor trying to do in the tutorial?

  A describe one selection technique
  B criticise traditional approaches to interviews
  C illustrate how she uses personality questionnaires

SECTION 4   *Questions 31–40*

Questions 31 and 32

Complete the notes below.

*Write **NO MORE THAN THREE WORDS AND/OR A NUMBER** for each answer.*

HAT-MAKING PROJECT
Project Profile

Example	Answer
Name of student:	Vivien

Type of school: 31 ....

Age of pupils: 32 ....

Questions 33 and 34

Label the diagrams.

*Write **NO MORE THAN THREE WORDS** for each answer.*

Introduction to Hat-Making

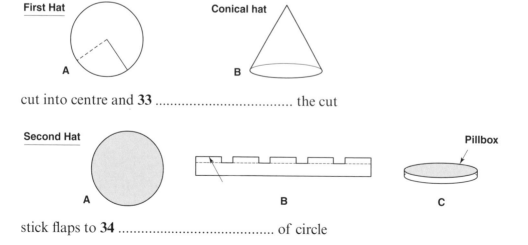

cut into centre and **33** .... the cut

stick flaps to **34** .... of circle

Questions 35–37

Complete the notes below.

Write **NO MORE THAN THREE WORDS** *for each answer.*

DESIGN PHASE

Stage A   Refer to research and design a hat 35 ....

Stage B   Make a small-scale 36 .... hat

Constraints

• material: paper

• colours: 37 ....

• glue: must not show

Questions 38–40

Indicate who made the hats below. Write the appropriate letter **A–E** *next to each name.*

38   Theresa ....

39   Muriel ....

40   Fabrice ....

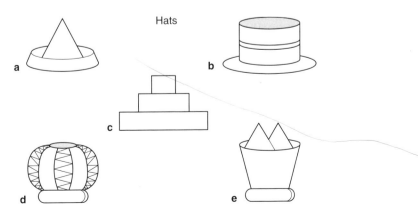

Hats

READING

READING PASSAGE 1

*You should spend about 20 minutes on **Questions 1–13** which are based on Reading Passage 1 below.*

A Remarkable Beetle

Some of the most remarkable beetles are the dung beetles, which spend almost their whole lives eating and breeding in dung[1].

More than 4,000 species of these remarkable creatures have evolved and adapted to the world's different climates and the dung of its many animals. Australia's native dung beetles are scrub and woodland dwellers, specialising in coarse marsupial droppings and avoiding the soft cattle dung in which bush flies and buffalo flies breed.

In the early 1960s George Bornemissza, then a scientist at the Australian Government's premier research organisation, the Commonwealth Scientific and Industrial Research Organisation (CSIRO), suggested that dung beetles should be introduced to Australia to control dung-breeding flies. Between 1968 and 1982, the CSIRO imported insects from about 50 different species of dung beetle, from Asia, Europe and Africa, aiming to match them to different climatic zones in Australia. Of the 26 species that are known to have become successfully integrated into the local environment, only one, an African species released in northern Australia, has reached its natural boundary.

Introducing dung beetles into a pasture is a simple process: approximately 1,500 beetles are released, a handful at a time, into fresh cow pats[2] in the cow pasture. The beetles immediately disappear beneath the pats digging and tunnelling and, if they successfully adapt to their new environment, soon become a permanent, self-sustaining part of the local ecology. In time they multiply and within three or four years the benefits to the pasture are obvious.

Dung beetles work from the inside of the pat so they are sheltered from predators such as birds and foxes. Most species burrow into the soil and bury dung in tunnels directly underneath the pats, which are hollowed out from within. Some large species originating from France excavate tunnels to a depth of approximately 30 cm below the dung pat. These beetles make sausage-shaped brood chambers along the tunnels. The shallowest tunnels belong to a much smaller Spanish species that buries dung in chambers that hang like fruit from the branches of a pear tree. South African beetles dig narrow tunnels of approximately 20 cm below the surface of the pat. Some surface-dwelling beetles, including a South African species, cut perfectly-shaped balls from the pat, which are rolled away and attached to the bases of plants.

For maximum dung burial in spring, summer and autumn, farmers require a variety of species with overlapping periods of activity. In the cooler environments of the state of Victoria, the large French species (2.5 cms long) is matched with smaller (half this size), temperate-climate Spanish species. The former are slow to recover from the winter cold and produce only one or two generations of offspring from late spring until autumn. The latter, which multiply rapidly in early spring, produce two to five generations annually. The South African ball-rolling species, being a sub-tropical beetle, prefers the climate of northern and coastal New South Wales where it commonly works with the South African tunnelling species. In warmer climates, many species are active for longer periods of the year.

Dung beetles were initially introduced in the late 1960s with a view to controlling buffalo flies by removing the dung within a day or two and so preventing flies from breeding. However, other benefits have become evident. Once the beetle larvae have finished pupation, the residue is a first-rate source of fertiliser. The tunnels abandoned by the beetles provide excellent aeration and water channels for root systems. In addition, when the new generation of beetles has left the nest the abandoned burrows are an attractive habitat for soil-enriching earthworms. The digested dung in these burrows is an excellent food supply for the earthworms, which decompose it further to provide essential soil nutrients. If it were not for the dung beetle, chemical fertiliser and dung would be washed by rain into streams and rivers before it could be absorbed into the hard earth, polluting water courses and causing blooms of blue-green algae. Without the beetles to dispose of the dung, cow pats would litter pastures making grass inedible to cattle and depriving the soil of sunlight. Australia's 30 million cattle each produce 10–12 cow pats a day. This amounts to 1.7 billion tonnes a year, enough to smother about 110,000 sq km of pasture, half the area of Victoria.

Dung beetles have become an integral part of the successful management of dairy farms in Australia over the past few decades. A number of species are available from the CSIRO or through a small number of private breeders, most of whom were entomologists with the CSIRO's dung beetle unit who have taken their specialised knowledge of the insect and opened small businesses in direct competition with their former employer.

Glossary
1. dung: the droppings or excreta of animals
2. cow pats: droppings of cows

Questions 1–5

Do the following statements reflect the claims of the writer in Reading Passage 1?

In boxes 1–5 on your answer sheet write

> **YES**　　　　　*if the statement reflects the claims of the writer*
> **NO**　　　　　*if the statement contradicts the claims of the writer*
> **NOT GIVEN**　*if it is impossible to say what the writer thinks about this*

1   Bush flies are easier to control than buffalo flies.

2   Four thousand species of dung beetle were initially brought to Australia by the CSIRO.

3   Dung beetles were brought to Australia by the CSIRO over a fourteen-year period.

4   At least twenty-six of the introduced species have become established in Australia.

5   The dung beetles cause an immediate improvement to the quality of a cow pasture.

Questions 6–8

Label the tunnels on the diagram below. Choose your labels from the box below the diagram.

Write your answers in boxes 6–8 on your answer sheet.

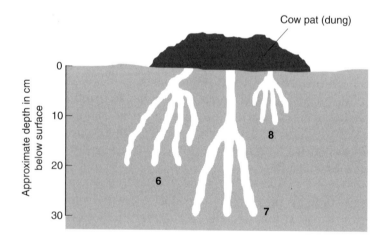

Dung Beetle Types	
French	Spanish
Mediterranean	South African
Australian native	South African ball roller

Question 9–13

Complete the table below.

Choose **NO MORE THAN THREE WORDS OR A NUMBER** *from Reading Passage 1 for each answer.*

Write your answers in boxes 9–13 on your answer sheet.

Species	Size	Preferred climate	Complementary species	Start of active period	Number of generations per year
French	2.5 cm	cool	Spanish	late spring	1–2
Spanish	1.25 cm	**9**		**10**	**11**
South African ball roller		**12**	**13**		

READING PASSAGE 2

*You should spend about 20 minutes on **Questions 14–28** which are based on Reading Passage 2 on the following pages.*

Questions 14–18

Reading Passage 2 has six sections **A–F**.

*Choose the most suitable headings for sections **A–D** and **F** from the list of headings below.*

*Write the appropriate numbers **i–ix** in boxes 14–18 on your answer sheet.*

	List of Headings
i	The probable effects of the new international trade agreement
ii	The environmental impact of modern farming
iii	Farming and soil erosion
iv	The effects of government policy in rich countries
v	Governments and management of the environment
vi	The effects of government policy in poor countries
vii	Farming and food output
viii	The effects of government policy on food output
ix	The new prospects for world trade

14   Section **A**

15   Section **B**

16   Section **C**

17   Section **D**

Example	Answer
Section **E**	**vi**

18   Section **F**

Section A

The role of governments in environmental management is difficult but inescapable. Sometimes, the state tries to manage the resources it owns, and does so badly. Often, however, governments act in an even more harmful way. They actually subsidise the exploitation and consumption of natural resources. A whole range of policies, from farm-price support to protection for coal-mining, do environmental damage and (often) make no economic sense. Scrapping them offers a two-fold bonus: a cleaner environment and a more efficient economy. Growth and environmentalism can actually go hand in hand, if politicians have the courage to confront the vested interest that subsidies create.

Section B

No activity affects more of the earth's surface than farming. It shapes a third of the planet's land area, not counting Antarctica, and the proportion is rising. World food output per head has risen by 4 per cent between the 1970s and 1980s mainly as a result of increases in yields from land already in cultivation, but also because more land has been brought under the plough. Higher yields have been achieved by increased irrigation, better crop breeding, and a doubling in the use of pesticides and chemical fertilisers in the 1970s and 1980s.

Section C

All these activities may have damaging environmental impacts. For example, land clearing for agriculture is the largest single cause of deforestation; chemical fertilisers and pesticides may contaminate water supplies; more intensive farming and the abandonment of fallow periods tend to exacerbate soil erosion; and the spread of monoculture and use of high-yielding varieties of crops have been accompanied by the disappearance of old varieties of food plants which might have provided some insurance against pests or diseases in future. Soil erosion threatens the productivity of land in both rich and poor countries. The United States, where the most careful measurements have been done, discovered in 1982 that about one-fifth of its farmland was losing topsoil at a rate likely to diminish the soil's productivity. The country subsequently embarked upon a program to convert 11 per cent of its cropped land to meadow or forest. Topsoil in India and China is vanishing much faster than in America.

Section D

Government policies have frequently compounded the environmental damage that farming can cause. In the rich countries, subsidies for growing crops and price supports for farm output drive up the price of land. The annual value of these subsidies is immense: about $250 billion, or more than all World Bank lending in the 1980s. To increase the output of crops per acre, a farmer's easiest option is to use more of the most readily available inputs: fertilisers and pesticides. Fertiliser use doubled in Denmark in the period 1960–1985 and increased in The Netherlands by 150 per cent. The quantity of pesticides applied has risen too: by 69 per cent in 1975–1984 in Denmark, for example, with a rise of 115 per cent in the frequency of application in the three years from 1981.

In the late 1980s and early 1990s some efforts were made to reduce farm subsidies. The most dramatic example was that of New Zealand, which scrapped most farm support in 1984. A study of the environmental effects, conducted in 1993, found that the end of fertiliser subsidies had been followed by a fall in fertiliser use (a fall compounded by the decline in world commodity prices, which cut farm incomes). The removal of subsidies also stopped land-clearing and over-stocking, which in the past had been the principal causes of erosion. Farms began to diversify. The one kind of subsidy whose removal appeared to have been bad for the environment was the subsidy to manage soil erosion.

In less enlightened countries, and in the European Union, the trend has been to reduce rather than eliminate subsidies, and to introduce new payments to encourage farmers to treat their land in environmentally friendlier ways, or to leave it fallow. It may sound strange but such payments need to be higher than the existing incentives for farmers to grow food crops. Farmers, however, dislike being paid to do nothing. In several countries they have become interested in the possibility of using fuel produced from crop residues either as a replacement for petrol (as ethanol) or as fuel for power stations (as biomass). Such fuels produce far less carbon dioxide than coal or oil, and absorb carbon dioxide as they grow. They are therefore less likely to contribute to the greenhouse effect. But they are rarely competitive with fossil fuels unless subsidised – and growing them does no less environmental harm than other crops.

Section E
In poor countries, governments aggravate other sorts of damage. Subsidies for pesticides and artificial fertilisers encourage farmers to use greater quantities than are needed to get the highest economic crop yield. A study by the International Rice Research Institute of pesticide use by farmers in South East Asia found that, with pest-resistant varieties of rice, even moderate applications of pesticide frequently cost farmers more than they saved. Such waste puts farmers on a chemical treadmill: bugs and weeds become resistant to poisons, so next year's poisons must be more lethal. One cost is to human health. Every year some 10,000 people die from pesticide poisoning, almost all of them in the developing countries, and another 400,000 become seriously ill. As for artificial fertilisers, their use world-wide increased by 40 per cent per unit of farmed land between the mid 1970s and late 1980s, mostly in the developing countries. Overuse of fertilisers may cause farmers to stop rotating crops or leaving their land fallow. That, in turn, may make soil erosion worse.

Section F
A result of the Uruguay Round of world trade negotiations is likely to be a reduction of 36 per cent in the average levels of farm subsidies paid by the rich countries in 1986–1990. Some of the world's food production will move from Western Europe to regions where subsidies are lower or non-existent, such as the former communist countries and parts of the developing world. Some environmentalists worry about this outcome. It will undoubtedly mean more pressure to convert natural habitat into farmland. But it will also have many desirable environmental effects. The intensity of farming in the rich world should decline, and the use of chemical inputs will diminish. Crops are more likely to be grown in the environments to which they are naturally suited. And more farmers in poor countries will have the money and the incentive to manage their land in ways that are sustainable in the long run. That is important. To feed an increasingly hungry world, farmers need every incentive to use their soil and water effectively and efficiently.

Questions 19–22

*Complete the table below using the information in sections **B** and **C** of Reading Passage 2.*

*Choose your answers **A**–**G** from the box below the table and write them in boxes 19–22 on your answer sheet.*

Agricultural practice	Environmental damage that may result
• **19**	• Deforestation
• **20**	• Degraded water supply
• More intensive farming	• **21**
• Expansion of monoculture	• **22**

A	Abandonment of fallow period
B	Disappearance of old plant varieties
C	Increased use of chemical inputs
D	Increased irrigation
E	Insurance against pests and diseases
F	Soil erosion
G	Clearing land for cultivation

Questions 23–27

*Choose the appropriate letters **A–D** and write them in boxes 23–27 on your answer sheet.*

23 Research completed in 1982 found that in the United States soil erosion

    A   reduced the productivity of farmland by 20 per cent.

    B   was almost as severe as in India and China.

    C   was causing significant damage to 20 per cent of farmland.

    D   could be reduced by converting cultivated land to meadow or forest.

24 By the mid-1980s, farmers in Denmark

    A   used 50 per cent less fertiliser than Dutch farmers.

    B   used twice as much fertiliser as they had in 1960.

    C   applied fertiliser much more frequently than in 1960.

    D   more than doubled the amount of pesticide they used in just 3 years.

25 Which one of the following increased in New Zealand after 1984?

    A   farm incomes

    B   use of fertiliser

    C   over-stocking

    D   farm diversification

26 The writer refers to some rich countries as being 'less enlightened' than New Zealand because

    A   they disapprove of paying farmers for *not* cultivating the land.

    B   their new fuel crops are as harmful as the ones they have replaced.

    C   their policies do not recognise the long-term benefit of ending subsidies.

    D   they have not encouraged their farmers to follow environmentally friendly practices.

27 The writer believes that the Uruguay Round agreements on trade will

    A   encourage more sustainable farming practices in the long term.

    B   do more harm than good to the international environment.

    C   increase pressure to cultivate land in the rich countries.

    D   be more beneficial to rich than to poor countries.

Question 28

From the list below choose the most suitable title for Reading Passage 2.

*Write the appropriate letter **A–E** in box 28 on your answer sheet.*

A   Environmental management

B   Increasing the world's food supply

C   Soil erosion

D   Fertilisers and pesticides – the way forward

E   Farm subsidies

READING PASSAGE 3

*You should spend about 20 minutes on **Questions 29–40** which are based on Reading Passage 3 below.*

THE CONCEPT OF ROLE THEORY

Role set

Any individual in any situation occupies a role in relation to other people. The particular individual with whom one is concerned in the analysis of any situation is usually given the name of *focal person*. He has the *focal role* and can be regarded as sitting in the middle of a group of people, with whom he interacts in some way in that situation. This group of people is called his *role set*. For instance, in the family situation, an individual's role set might be shown as in *Figure 6*.

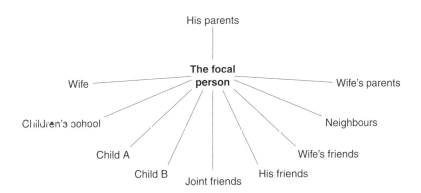

Figure 6

The role set should include all those with whom the individual has more than trivial interactions.

Role definition

The definition of any individual's role in any situation will be a combination of the *role expectations* that the members of the role set have of the focal role. These expectations are often occupationally defined, sometimes even legally so. The role definitions of lawyers and doctors are fairly clearly defined both in legal and in cultural terms. The role definitions of, say, a film star or bank manager, are also fairly clearly defined in cultural terms, too clearly perhaps.

Individuals often find it hard to escape from the role that cultural traditions have defined for them. Not only with doctors or lawyers is the required role behaviour so constrained that if you are in that role for long it eventually becomes part of *you*, part of your personality. Hence, there is *some* likelihood that all accountants *will* be alike or that all blondes are similar – they are forced that way by the expectations of their role.

It is often important that you make it clear what your particular role is at a given time. The means of doing this are called, rather obviously, *role signs*. The simplest of role signs is a uniform. The number of stripes on your arm or pips on your shoulder is a very precise role definition which allows you to do certain very prescribed things in certain situations. Imagine yourself questioning a stranger on a dark street at midnight without wearing the role signs of a policeman!

In social circumstances, dress has often been used as a role sign to indicate the nature and degree of formality of any gathering and occasionally the social status of people present. The current trend towards blurring these role signs in dress is probably democratic, but it also makes some people very insecure. Without role signs, who is to know who has what role?

Place is another role sign. Managers often behave very differently outside the office and in it, even to the same person. They use a change of location to indicate a change in role from, say, boss to friend. Indeed, if you wish to change your roles you must find some outward sign that you are doing so or you won't be permitted to change – the subordinate will continue to hear you as his boss no matter how hard you try to be his friend. In very significant cases of role change, e.g. from a soldier in the ranks to officer, from bachelor to married man, the change of role has to have a very obvious *sign*, hence *rituals*. It is interesting to observe, for instance, some decline in the emphasis given to marriage rituals. This could be taken as an indication that there is no longer such a big change in role from single to married person, and therefore no need for a public change in *sign*.

In organisations, office signs and furniture are often used as role signs. These and other perquisites of status are often frowned upon, but they may serve a purpose as a kind of uniform in a democratic society; roles without signs often lead to confused or differing expectations of the role of the focal person.

Role ambiguity
Role ambiguity results when there is some uncertainty in the minds, either of the focal person or of the members of his role set, as to precisely what his role is at any given time. One of the crucial expectations that shape the role definition is that of the individual, the focal person himself. If his occupation of the role is unclear, or if it differs from that of the others in the role set, there will be a degree of role ambiguity. Is this bad? Not necessarily, for the ability to shape one's own role is one of the freedoms that many people desire, but the ambiguity may lead

to role stress which will be discussed later on. The virtue of job descriptions is that they lessen this role ambiguity. Unfortunately, job descriptions are seldom complete role definitions, except at the lower end of the scale. At middle and higher management levels, they are often a list of formal jobs and duties that say little about the more subtle and informal expectations of the role. The result is therefore to give the individual an uncomfortable feeling that there are things left unsaid, i.e. to *heighten* the sense of role ambiguity.

Looking at role ambiguity from the other side, from the point of view of the members of the role set, lack of clarity in the role of the focal person can cause insecurity, lack of confidence, irritation and even anger among members of his role set. One list of the roles of a manager identified the following: executive, planner, policy maker, expert, controller of rewards and punishments, counsellor, friend, teacher. If it is not clear, through role signs of one sort or another, which role is currently the operational one, the other party may not react in the appropriate way – we may, in fact, hear quite another message if the focal person speaks to us, for example, as a teacher and we hear her as an executive.

Questions 29–35

Do the following statements reflect the views of the writer in Reading Passage 3?

In boxes 29–35 on your answer sheet write

> **YES**   *if the statement reflects the views of the writer*
> **NO**   *if the statement contradicts the views of the writer*
> **NOT GIVEN**   *if it is impossible to know what the writer thinks about this*

29   It would be a good idea to specify the role definitions of soldiers more clearly

30   Accountants may be similar to one another because they have the same type of job.

31   It is probably a good idea to keep dress as a role sign even nowadays.

32   The decline in emphasis on marriage rituals should be reversed.

33   Today furniture operates as a role sign in the same way as dress has always done.

34   It is a good idea to remove role ambiguity.

35   Job descriptions eliminate role ambiguity for managers.

Questions 36–39

*Choose **ONE OR TWO WORDS** from Reading Passage 3 for each answer.*

Write your answers in boxes 36–39 on your answer sheet.

36 A new headmaster of a school who enlarges his office and puts in expensive carpeting is using the office as a ...

37 The graduation ceremony in many universities is an important ...

38 The wig which judges wear in UK courts is a ...

39 The parents of students in a school are part of the headmaster's ...

Question 40

*Choose the appropriate letter **A–D** and write it in box 40 on your answer sheet.*

This text is taken from

    A   a guide for new managers in a company.
    B   a textbook analysis of behaviour in organisations.
    C   a critical study of the importance of role signs in modern society.
    D   a newspaper article about role changes.

WRITING

WRITING TASK 1

You should spend about 20 minutes on this task.

> *The chart below shows the amount spent on six consumer goods in four European countries.*
>
> *Write a report for a university lecturer describing the information shown below.*

You should write at least 150 words.

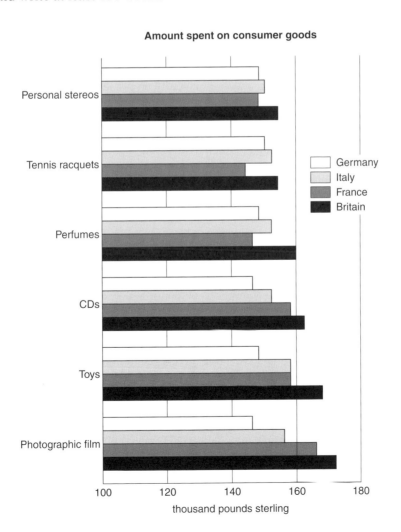

Amount spent on consumer goods

WRITING TASK 2

You should spend about 40 minutes on this task.

Present a written argument or case to an educated reader with no specialist knowledge of the following topic.

> *When a country develops its technology, the traditional skills and ways of*
> *life die out. It is pointless to try and keep them alive.*
>
> *To what extent do you agree or disagree with this opinion?*

You should use your own ideas, knowledge and experience and support your arguments with examples and relevant evidence.

You should write at least 250 words.

SPEAKING

PART 1

The examiner asks the candidate about him/herself, his/her home, work or studies and other familiar topics.

EXAMPLE

Festivals

- Tell me about the most important festival in your country.
- What special food and activities are connected with this festival?
- What do you most enjoy about it?
- Do you think festivals are important for a country? [Why?]

PART 2

> **Describe a film or a TV programme which has made a strong impression on you.**
> **You should say:**
> > **what kind of film or TV programme it was, e.g. comedy**
> > **when you saw the film or TV programme**
> > **what the film or TV programme was about**
> **and explain why this film or TV programme made such an impression on you.**

You will have to talk about the topic for 1 to 2 minutes. You have one minute to think about what you're going to say. You can make some notes to help you if you wish.

PART 3

Discussion topics:

People's cinema-going habits nowadays

Example questions:
Do you think the cinema has increased or decreased in popularity in recent years?
In your opinion, will this trend continue into the future?

Making a film or TV drama of real/fictional events

Example questions:
What are the advantages and disadvantages of making films of real-life events?
How important do you think it is for a film-maker to remain true to the original story?

Censorship and the freedom of the film-maker/TV producer

Example questions:
Should films and television be censored or should we be free to choose what we see?
How do you think censorship laws will change in the next 20 years?

Test 3

SECTION 1   *Questions 1–10*

Complete the notes below.

*Write **NO MORE THAN THREE WORDS AND/OR A NUMBER** for each answer.*

NOTES – Christmas Dinner

Example	Answer
Number to book for:	...**45**..........

Date of dinner: 21 December

Choices for venue:

- First choice   **1** ....   Tel. number: not known
- Second choice   **2** ....   Tel. number: 777192
- Third choice   **3** ....   Tel. number: **4** ....

Price per person: £12

Restaurant must have vegetarian food and a **5** ....

Menu: First course - French Onion Soup OR Fruit Juice

       Main course - Roast Dinner   OR **6** ....

       Dessert   - Plum Pudding   OR Apple Pie

                   - Coffee

Restaurant requires from us:

    7 .... and letter of confirmation

    and we must **8** .... in advance.

Must confirm in writing by: **9** ....

Put notice in **10** ....

SECTION 2   *Questions 11–20*

Questions 11–13

Complete the table below.

*Write **NO MORE THAN THREE WORDS OR A NUMBER** for each answer.*

MEMBERSHIP OF SPORTS CENTRE	
Cost	**11** £ .... per **12** ....
Where?	**13** ....
When?	2 to 6 pm, Monday to Thursday
Bring:	Union card Photo Fee

Questions 14–16

Complete the table below.

*Write **NO MORE THAN THREE WORDS** for each answer.*

Always bring sports **14** .... when you come to **15** .... or use the Centre's facilities.	
Opening hours	9 am to 10 pm on **16** .... 10 am to 6 pm on Saturdays
50% 'morning discount'	9 am to 12 noon on weekdays

Questions 17–20

Look at the map of the Sports Complex below.

Label the buildings on the map of the Sports Complex.

Choose your answers from the box below and write them against Questions 17–20.

Arts Studio
Football Pitch
Tennis Courts
Dance Studio
Fitness Room
Reception
Squash Courts

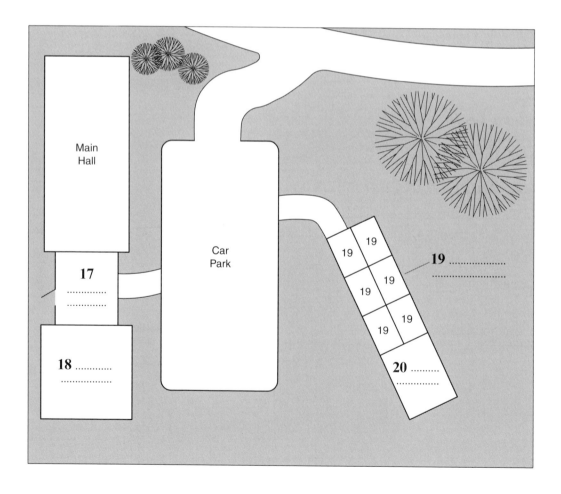

SECTION 3   *Questions 21–30*

Complete the form below.

*Write **NO MORE THAN THREE WORDS AND/OR NUMBER** for each answer.*

YOUNG ELECTRONIC ENGINEER COMPETITION

Name(s) of designer(s): John Brown

21 ....

Age: **22** ....

Name of design: **23** ....

Dimensions of equipment: **24**

Width	Length	Depth
.... cm	.... cm	.... cm

Power: Battery

Special features: **25** ....

26 ....

27 ....

Cost: parts $5

28 .... $9.50

Other comments: need help to make **29** ....

would like to develop range of sizes

Send by: **30** ....

SECTION 4   *Questions 31–40*

Questions 31–33

Complete the table below.

Write **NO MORE THAN TWO WORDS** *for each answer.*

"NEW" MEAT	CAN BE COMPARED TO	PROBLEM
kangaroo	**31**	**32** ....
crocodile	chicken	fatty
ostrich	**33**	

Questions 34–36

Complete the table below.

Write **NO MORE THAN THREE WORDS** *for each answer.*

OSTRICH PRODUCT	USE
Ostrich feathers	• tribal ceremonial dress • **34** .... • decorated hats
Ostrich hide	• **35** ....
Ostrich **36**	• 'biltong'

Questions 37–40

Choose the correct letters A–C.

37 Ostrich meat

    A   has more protein than beef.
    B   tastes nearly as good as beef.
    C   is very filling.

38 One problem with ostrich farming in Britain is

    A   the climate.
    B   the cost of transporting birds.
    C   the price of ostrich eggs.

39 Ostrich chicks reared on farms

    A   must be kept in incubators until mature.
    B   are very independent.
    C   need looking after carefully.

40 The speaker suggests ostrich farms are profitable because

    A   little initial outlay is required.
    B   farmed birds are very productive.
    C   there is a good market for the meat.

READING PASSAGE 1

*You should spend about 20 minutes on **Questions 1–12** which are based on Reading Passage 1 below.*

THE DEPARTMENT OF ETHNOGRAPHY

The Department of Ethnography was created as a separate department within the British Museum in 1946, after 140 years of gradual development from the original Department of Antiquities. It is concerned with the people of Africa, the Americas, Asia, the Pacific and parts of Europe. While this includes complex kingdoms, as in Africa, and ancient empires, such as those of the Americas, the primary focus of attention in the twentieth century has been on small-scale societies. Through its collections, the Department's specific interest is to document how objects are created and used, and to understand their importance and significance to those who produce them. Such objects can include both the extraordinary and the mundane, the beautiful and the banal.

The collections of the Department of Ethnography include approximately 300,000 artefacts, of which about half are the product of the present century. The Department has a vital role to play in providing information on non-Western cultures to visitors and scholars. To this end, the collecting emphasis has often been less on individual objects than on groups of material which allow the display of a broad range of a society's cultural expressions.

Much of the more recent collecting was carried out in the field, sometimes by Museum staff working on general anthropological projects in collaboration with a wide variety of national governments and other institutions. The material collected includes great technical series – for instance, of textiles from Bolivia, Guatemala, Indonesia and areas of West Africa – or of artefact types such as boats. The latter include working examples of coracles from India, reed boats from Lake Titicaca in the Andes, kayaks from the Arctic, and dug-out canoes from several countries. The field assemblages, such as those from the Sudan, Madagascar and Yemen, include a whole range of material culture representative of one people. This might cover the necessities of life of an African herdsman or an Arabian farmer, ritual objects, or even on occasion airport art. Again, a series of acquisitions might represent a decade's fieldwork documenting social experience as expressed in the varieties of clothing and jewellery styles, tents and camel trappings from various Middle Eastern countries, or in the developing preferences in personal adornment and dress from Papua New Guinea. Particularly interesting are a series of collections which continue to document the evolution of ceremony and of material forms for which the Department already possesses early (if not the earliest) collections formed after the first contact with Europeans.

The importance of these acquisitions extends beyond the objects themselves. They come to the Museum with documentation of the social context, ideally including photographic records. Such acquisitions have multiple purposes. Most significantly they document for future change. Most people think of the cultures represented in the collection in terms of the absence of advanced technology. In fact, traditional practices draw on a continuing wealth of technological ingenuity. Limited resources and ecological constraints are often overcome by personal skills that would be regarded as exceptional in the West. Of growing interest is the way in which much of what we might see as disposable is, elsewhere, recycled and reused.

With the independence of much of Asia and Africa after 1945, it was assumed that economic progress would rapidly lead to the disappearance or assimilation of many small-scale societies. Therefore, it was felt that the Museum should acquire materials representing people whose art or material culture, ritual or political structures were on the point of irrevocable change. This attitude altered with the realisation that marginal communities can survive and adapt in spite of partial integration into a notoriously fickle world economy. Since the seventeenth century, with the advent of trading companies exporting manufactured textiles to North America and Asia, the importation of cheap goods has often contributed to the destruction of local skills and indigenous markets. On the one hand modern imported goods may be used in an everyday setting, while on the other hand other traditional objects may still be required for ritually significant events. Within this context trade and exchange attitudes are inverted. What are utilitarian objects to a Westerner may be prized objects in other cultures – when transformed by local ingenuity – principally for aesthetic value. In the same way, the West imports goods from other peoples and in certain circumstances categorises them as 'art'.

Collections act as an ever-expanding database, not merely for scholars and anthropologists, but for people involved in a whole range of educational and artistic purposes. These include schools and universities as well as colleges of art and design. The provision of information about non-Western aesthetics and techniques, not just for designers and artists but for all visitors, is a growing responsibility for a Department whose own context is an increasingly multicultural European society.

Questions 1–6

Do the following statements agree with the information given in Reading Passage 1?

In boxes 1–6 on your answer sheet write

> **TRUE**   *if the statement is true according to the passage*
> **FALSE**   *if the statement is false according to the passage*
> **NOT GIVEN** *if the information is not given in the passage*

Example	Answer
The Department of Ethnography replaced the Department of Antiquities at the British Museum.	**FALSE**

1   The twentieth-century collections come mainly from mainstream societies such as the US and Europe.

2   The Department of Ethnography focuses mainly on modern societies.

3   The Department concentrates on collecting single unrelated objects of great value.

4   The textile collection of the Department of Ethnography is the largest in the world.

5   Traditional societies are highly inventive in terms of technology.

6   Many small-scale societies have survived and adapted in spite of predictions to the contrary.

Questions 7–12

Some of the exhibits at the Department of Ethnography are listed below (Questions 7–12).

The writer gives these exhibits as examples of different collection types.

Match each exhibit with the collection type with which it is associated in Reading Passage 1.

Write the appropriate letters in boxes 7–12 on your answer sheet.

NB You may use any collection type more than once.

	Collection Types
AT	Artefact Types
EC	Evolution of Ceremony
FA	Field Assemblages
SE	Social Experience
TS	Technical Series

Example	*Answer*
Boats	**AT**

7   Bolivian textiles

8   Indian coracles

9   airport art

10 Arctic kayaks

11 necessities of life of an Arabian farmer

12 tents from the Middle East

READING PASSAGE 2

*You should spend about 20 minutes on **Questions 13–25** which are based on Reading Passage 2 on the following pages.*

Questions 13–15

Reading Passage 2 has six sections **A–F**.

*Choose the most suitable headings for sections **A**, **B** and **D** from the list of headings below.*

*Write the appropriate numbers **i–vii** in boxes 13–15 on your answer sheet.*

List of Headings
i   Amazonia as unable to sustain complex societies
ii The role of recent technology in ecological research in Amazonia
iii The hostility of the indigenous population to North American influences
iv Recent evidence
v   Early research among the Indian Amazons
vi The influence of prehistoric inhabitants on Amazonian natural history
vii The great difficulty of changing local attitudes and practices

13   Section **A**

14   Section **B**

Example	*Answer*
Section **C**	**iv**

15   Section **D**

Secrets of the Forest

A In 1942 Allan R Holmberg, a doctoral student in anthropology from Yale University, USA, ventured deep into the jungle of Bolivian Amazonia and searched out an isolated band of Siriono Indians. The Siriono, Holmberg later wrote, led a "strikingly backward" existence. Their villages were little more than clusters of thatched huts. Life itself was a perpetual and punishing search for food: some families grew *manioc* and other starchy crops in small garden plots cleared from the forest, while other members of the tribe scoured the country for small game and promising fish holes. When local resources became depleted, the tribe moved on. As for technology, Holmberg noted, the Siriono "may be classified among the most handicapped peoples of the world". Other than bows, arrows and crude digging sticks, the only tools the Siriono seemed to possess were "two machetes worn to the size of pocket-knives".

B Although the lives of the Siriono have changed in the intervening decades, the image of them as Stone Age relics has endured. Indeed, in many respects the Siriono epitomize the popular conception of life in Amazonia. To casual observers, as well as to influential natural scientists and regional planners, the luxuriant forests of Amazonia seem ageless, unconquerable, a habitat totally hostile to human civilization. The apparent simplicity of Indian ways of life has been judged an evolutionary adaptation to forest ecology, living proof that Amazonia could not – and cannot – sustain a more complex society. Archaeological traces of far more elaborate cultures have been dismissed as the ruins of invaders from outside the region, abandoned to decay in the uncompromising tropical environment.

C The popular conception of Amazonia and its native residents would be enormously consequential if it were true. But the human history of Amazonia in the past 11,000 years betrays that view as myth. Evidence gathered in recent years from anthropology and archaeology indicates that the region has supported a series of indigenous cultures for eleven thousand years; an extensive network of complex societies – some with populations perhaps as large as 100,000 – thrived there for more than 1,000 years before the arrival of Europeans. (Indeed, some contemporary tribes, including the Siriono, still live among the earthworks of earlier cultures.) Far from being evolutionarily retarded, prehistoric Amazonian people developed technologies and cultures that were advanced for their time. If the lives of Indians today seem "primitive", the appearance is not the result of some environmental adaptation or ecological barrier; rather it is a comparatively recent adaptation to centuries of economic and political pressure. Investigators who argue otherwise have unwittingly projected the present onto the past.

D The evidence for a revised view of Amazonia will take many people by surprise. Ecologists have assumed that tropical ecosystems were shaped entirely by natural forces and they have focused their research on habitats they believe have escaped human influence. But as the University of Florida ecologist, Peter Feinsinger, has noted, an approach that leaves people out of the equation is no longer tenable. The archaeological evidence shows that the natural history of Amazonia is to a surprising extent tied to the activities of its prehistoric inhabitants.

E The realization comes none too soon. In June 1992 political and environmental leaders from across the world met in Rio de Janeiro to discuss how developing countries can advance their economies without destroying their natural resources. The challenge is especially difficult in Amazonia. Because the tropical forest has been depicted as ecologically unfit for large-scale human occupation, some environmentalists have opposed development of any kind. Ironically, one major casualty of that extreme position has been the environment itself. While policy makers struggle to define and implement appropriate legislation, development of the most destructive kind has continued apace over vast areas.

F The other major casualty of the "naturalism" of environmental scientists has been the indigenous Amazonians, whose habits of hunting, fishing, and slash-and-burn cultivation often have been represented as harmful to the habitat. In the clash between environmentalists and developers, the Indians, whose presence is in fact crucial to the survival of the forest, have suffered the most. The new understanding of the pre-history of Amazonia, however, points toward a middle ground. Archaeology makes clear that with judicious management selected parts of the region could support more people than anyone thought before. The long-buried past, it seems, offers hope for the future.

Questions 16–21

Do the following statements agree with the views of the writer in Reading Passage 2?

In boxes 16–21 on your answer sheet write

> **YES** *if the statement agrees with the views of the writer*
> **NO** *if the statement contradicts the views of the writer*
> **NOT GIVEN** *if it is impossible to say what the writer thinks about this*

Example	*Answer*
The prehistoric inhabitants of Amazonia were relatively backward in technological terms.	**NO**

16 The reason for the simplicity of the Indian way of life is that Amazonia has always been unable to support a more complex society.

17 There is a crucial popular misconception about the human history of Amazonia.

18 There are lessons to be learned from similar ecosystems in other parts of the world.

19 Most ecologists were aware that the areas of Amazonia they were working in had been shaped by human settlement.

20 The indigenous Amazonian Indians are necessary to the well-being of the forest.

21 It would be possible for certain parts of Amazonia to support a higher population.

Questions 22–25

*Choose the appropriate letters **A–D** and write them in boxes 22–25 on your answer sheet.*

22 In 1942 the US anthropology student concluded that the Siriono

    A   were unusually aggressive and cruel.
    B   had had their way of life destroyed by invaders.
    C   were an extremely primitive society.
    D   had only recently made permanent settlements.

23 The author believes recent discoveries of the remains of complex societies in Amazonia
    A   are evidence of early indigenous communities.
    B   are the remains of settlements by invaders.
    C   are the ruins of communities established since the European invasions.
    D   show the region has only relatively recently been covered by forest.

24 The assumption that the tropical ecosystem of Amazonia has been created solely by natural forces
    A   has often been questioned by ecologists in the past.
    B   has been shown to be incorrect by recent research.
    C   was made by Peter Feinsinger and other ecologists.
    D   has led to some fruitful discoveries.

25 The application of our new insights into the Amazonian past would

    A   warn us against allowing any development at all.
    B   cause further suffering to the Indian communities.
    C   change present policies on development in the region.
    D   reduce the amount of hunting, fishing, and 'slash-and-burn'.

READING PASSAGE 3

*You should spend about 20 minutes on **Questions 26–40** which are based on Reading Passage 3 below.*

HIGHS & LOWS

Hormone levels – and hence our moods – may be affected by the weather. Gloomy weather can cause depression, but sunshine appears to raise the spirits. In Britain, for example, the dull weather of winter drastically cuts down the amount of sunlight that is experienced which strongly affects some people. They become so depressed and lacking in energy that their work and social life are affected. This condition has been given the name SAD (Seasonal Affective Disorder). Sufferers can fight back by making the most of any sunlight in winter and by spending a few hours each day under special, full-spectrum lamps. These provide more ultraviolet and blue-green light than ordinary fluorescent and tungsten lights. Some Russian scientists claim that children learn better after being exposed to ultraviolet light. In warm countries, hours of work are often arranged so that workers can take a break, or even a siesta, during the hottest part of the day. Scientists are working to discover the links between the weather and human beings' moods and performance.

It is generally believed that tempers grow shorter in hot, muggy weather. There is no doubt that 'crimes against the person' rise in the summer, when the weather is hotter and fall in the winter when the weather is colder. Research in the United States has shown a relationship between temperature and street riots. The frequency of riots rises dramatically as the weather gets warmer, hitting a peak around 27–30°C. But is this effect really due to a mood change caused by the heat? Some scientists argue that trouble starts more often in hot weather merely because there are more people in the street when the weather is good.

Psychologists have also studied how being cold affects performance. Researchers compared divers working in icy cold water at 5°C with others in water at 20°C (about swimming pool temperature). The colder water made the divers worse at simple arithmetic and other mental tasks. But significantly, their performance was impaired as soon as they were put into the cold water – before their bodies had time to cool down. This suggests that the low temperature did not slow down mental functioning directly, but the feeling of cold distracted the divers from their tasks.

Psychologists have conducted studies showing that people become less sceptical and more optimistic when the weather is sunny. However, this apparently does not just depend on the temperature. An American psychologist studied customers in a temperature-controlled restaurant. They gave bigger tips when the sun was shining and smaller tips when it wasn't, even though the temperature in the restaurant was the same. A link between weather and mood is made believable by the evidence for a connection between behaviour and the length of the daylight hours. This in turn might involve the level of a hormone called melatonin, produced in the pineal gland in the brain. The amount of melatonin falls with greater exposure to daylight. Research shows that melatonin plays an important part in the seasonal behaviour of certain animals. For example, food consumption of stags increases during the winter, reaching a peak in February/March. It falls again to a low point in May, then rises to a peak in September, before dropping to another minimum in November. These changes seem to be triggered by varying melatonin levels.

In the laboratory, hamsters put on more weight when the nights are getting shorter and their melatonin levels are falling. On the other hand, if they are given injections of melatonin, they will stop eating altogether. It seems that time cues provided by the changing lengths of day and night trigger changes in animals' behaviour – changes that are needed to cope with the cycle of the seasons. People's moods too, have been shown to react to the length of the daylight hours. Sceptics might say that longer exposure to sunshine puts people in a better mood because they associate it with the happy feelings of holidays and freedom from responsibility. However, the belief that rain and murky weather make people more unhappy is borne out by a study in Belgium, which showed that a telephone counselling service gets more telephone calls from people with suicidal feelings when it rains.

When there is a thunderstorm brewing, some people complain of the air being 'heavy' and of feeling irritable, moody and on edge. They may be reacting to the fact that the air can become slightly positively charged when large thunderclouds are generating the intense electrical fields that cause lightning flashes. The positive charge increases the levels of serotonin (a chemical involved in sending signals in the nervous system). High levels of serotonin in certain areas of the nervous system make people more active and reactive and, possibly, more aggressive. When certain winds are blowing, such as the Mistral in southern France and the Föhn in southern Germany, mood can be affected – and the number of traffic accidents rises. It may be significant that the concentration of positively charged particles is greater than normal in these winds. In the United Kingdom, 400,000 ionizers are sold every year. These small machines raise the number of negative ions in the air in a room. Many people claim they feel better in negatively charged air.

Questions 26–28

Choose the appropriate letters A–D and write them in boxes 26–28 on your answer sheet.

26 Why did the divers perform less well in colder conditions?

    A   They were less able to concentrate.
    B   Their body temperature fell too quickly.
    C   Their mental functions were immediately affected by the cold.
    D   They were used to swimming pool conditions.

27 The number of daylight hours

    A   affects the performance of workers in restaurants.
    B   influences animal feeding habits.
    C   makes animals like hamsters more active.
    D   prepares humans for having greater leisure time.

28 Human irritability may be influenced by

    A   how nervous and aggressive people are.
    B   reaction to certain weather phenomena.
    C   the number of ions being generated by machines.
    D   the attitude of people to thunderstorms.

Questions 29–34

Do the following statements agree with the information in Reading Passage 3?

In boxes 29–34 on your answer sheet write

    TRUE   *if the statement is true according to the passage*
    FALSE   *if the statement is false according to the passage*
    NOT GIVEN *if the information is not given in the passage*

29 Seasonal Affective Disorder is disrupting children's education in Russia.

30 Serotonin is an essential cause of human aggression.

31 Scientific evidence links 'happy associations with weather' to human mood.

32 A link between depression and the time of year has been established.

33 Melatonin levels increase at certain times of the year.

34 Positively charged ions can influence eating habits.

Questions 35–37

According to the text which **THREE** of the following conditions have been scientifically proved to have a psychological effect on humans?

*Choose **THREE** letters **A–G** and write them in boxes 35–37 on your answer sheet.*

A   lack of negative ions
B   rainy weather
C   food consumption
D   high serotonin levels
E   sunny weather
F   freedom from worry
G   lack of counselling facilities

Questions 38–40

Complete each of the following statements with the best ending from the box below.

*Write the appropriate letters **A–G** in boxes 38–40 on your answer sheet.*

38   It has been established that social tension increases significantly in the United States during …

39   Research has shown that a hamster's bodyweight increases according to its exposure to …

40   Animals cope with changing weather and food availability because they are influenced by …

A   daylight
B   hot weather
C   melatonin
D   moderate temperatures
E   poor co-ordination
F   time cues
G   impaired performance

WRITING

WRITING TASK 1

You should spend about 20 minutes on this task.

> *The charts below show the levels of participation in education and science in developing and industrialised countries in 1980 and 1990.*
>
> *Write a report for a university lecturer describing the information shown below.*

You should write at least 150 words.

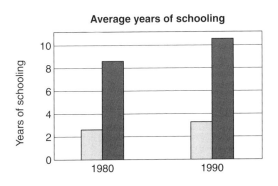

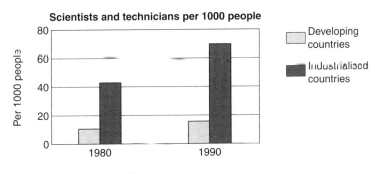

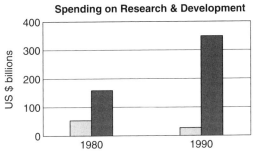

WRITING TASK 2

You should spend about 40 minutes on this task.

Present a written argument or case to an educated reader with no specialist knowledge of the following topic.

>*In many countries children are engaged in some kind of paid work. Some people regard this as completely wrong, while others consider it as valuable work experience, important for learning and taking responsibility.*
>
>*What are your opinions on this?*

You should use your own ideas, knowledge and experience and support your arguments with examples and relevant evidence.

You should write at least 250 words.

SPEAKING

PART 1

The examiner asks the candidate about him/herself, his/her home, work or studies and other familiar topics.

EXAMPLE

Visitors

- What would you suggest a visitor should see and do in your country?
- Are there any traditional arts or music you would recommend?
- Tell me about the kind of foreign visitors or tourists who go to your country.
- In what ways has tourism changed your country?

PART 2

Describe a memorable event in your life.
You should say:
   when the event took place
   where the event took place
   what happened exactly
and explain why this event was memorable for you.

You will have to talk about the topic for 1 to 2 minutes. You have one minute to think about what you're going to say.
You can make some notes to help you if you wish.

PART 3

Discussion topics:

The role of ceremony in our lives

Example questions:
How important are ceremonies in our lives?
Do you see the role of private and public ceremonies changing in the future?

Attitudes to marriage in your country

Example questions:
Have attitudes to marriage changed in recent years?
In what ways do men and women feel differently about marriage, in your opinion?

Events of national/global significance

Example questions:
What sort of national events make headlines in your country?
Does the media in your country pay more attention to global or national events?

Test 4

SECTION 1   Questions 1–10

Questions 1 and 2

Complete the form opposite.

*Write **NO MORE THAN THREE WORDS AND/OR A NUMBER** for each answer.*

Birth Statistics	
Example Date of birth:	Answer 10 August
Sex:	male
First name:	Tom
Surname:	Lightfoot
Weight:	1 .... kgs
Length:	2 .... cms
Colour of hair:	black

Questions 3–5

Label the map. Choose your answers from the box below.

*Write the appropriate letters **A–E** on the map.*

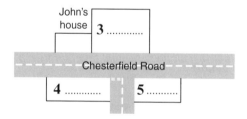

```
A   State Bank
B   St George's Hospital
C   Garage
D   Library
E   University
```

Questions 6–10

*Write **NO MORE THAN THREE WORDS OR A NUMBER** for each answer.*

	Gift for Susan	Gift for baby
What will they buy?	**6**	**7** ....
Where will they buy the gifts?	**8**	**9** ....
Approximate prices?	$15	**10** $ ....

SECTION 2   *Questions 11–20*

Complete the table below.

*Write **NO MORE THAN THREE WORDS** for each answer.*

For the recommendation column, write

  A   You **must** buy this.

  B   **Maybe** you should buy this.

  C   You **should never** buy this.

Name	Advantage(s)	Disadvantage(s)	Recommendation
Unbreakable Vacuum Flask	• Contains no **11** .... • Steel guaranteed for 20 years • Keeps warm for **12**	• Expensive • Leaves **13**	B
Whistle Key Holder	• Press-button light useful for finding keyhole • **14**	• Unpleasant noise • Doesn't work through **15**	**16** ....
Army Flashlight (squeeze light)	• Useful for **17** .... • Works **18**	• Has **19**	C
Decoy Camera (to trick burglars)	• Realistic **20**	• Difficult to fix onto wall	A

SECTION 3   *Questions 21–30*

Questions 21–23

Choose the correct letters A–C.

21 Amina's project is about a local

    A   school.
    B   hospital.
    C   factory.

22 Dr Bryson particularly liked

    A   the introduction.
    B   the first chapter.
    C   the middle section.

23 Amina was surprised because she

    A   thought it was bad.
    B   wrote it quickly.
    C   found it difficult to do.

Questions 24–26

What suggestions does Dr Bryson make?

Complete the table as follows.

    Write A   *if he says* **KEEP UNCHANGED**
    Write B   *if he says* **REWRITE**
    Write C   *if he says* **REMOVE COMPLETELY**

Example	*Answer*
Section headings	**B**

Information on housing	**24**	....
Interview data	**25**	....
Chronology	**26**	....

Questions 27–30

Complete the notes below.

*Write **NO MORE THAN THREE WORDS AND/OR A NUMBER** for each answer.*

SCHEDULE OF ACTION

- Read 'Approaches to Local History'
  by John Mervis.

- Read **27** '.................................,'
  by Kate Oakwell.

- Make changes and show to
  28 ....

- Do **29** ....
  by 29 June.

- Laser print before **30** ....

- Hand in to Faculty Office.

SECTION 4   *Questions 31–40*

Questions 31–34

Write **NUMBERS AND/OR NO MORE THAN FOUR WORDS** *for each answer.*

31   Between what times is the road traffic lightest?

    ....

32   Who will notice the noise most?

    ....

33   Which day of the week has the least traffic?

    ....

34   What will be the extra cost of modifying houses?

    ....

Question 35

Choose the correct letter **A–D**.

The noise levels at the site can reach

> **A**   45 decibels.
> **B**   55 decibels.
> **C**   67 decibels.
> **D**   70 decibels.

Questions 36–38

Complete the table showing where devices used in reducing noise could be fitted in the houses.

Write: **W**   for walls
         D   for doors
         C   for ceilings

Example		Answer
	acoustic seals	**D**

36	double thickness plaster board	
37	mechanical ventilation	
38	air conditioning	

Questions 39 and 40

Choose the correct letters A–D.

39   Which is the correct construction for acoustic double glazing?

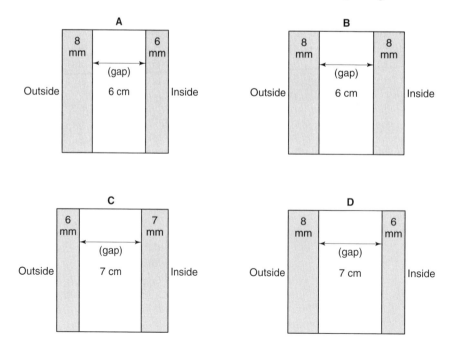

40   What is the best layout for the houses?

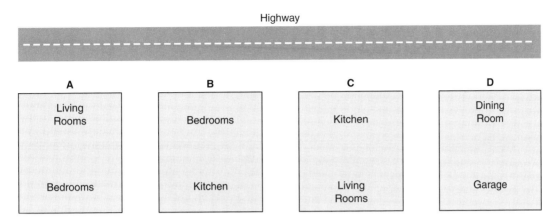

READING

READING PASSAGE 1

*You should spend about 20 minutes on **Questions 1–13** which are based on Reading Passage 1 below.*

Part One

A   Air pollution is increasingly becoming the focus of government and citizen concern around the globe. From Mexico City and New York, to Singapore and Tokyo, new solutions to this old problem are being proposed, trialled and implemented with ever increasing speed. It is feared that unless pollution reduction measures are able to keep pace with the continued pressures of urban growth, air quality in many of the world's major cities will deteriorate beyond reason.

B   Action is being taken along several fronts: through new legislation, improved enforcement and innovative technology. In Los Angeles, state regulations are forcing manufacturers to try to sell ever cleaner cars: their first of the cleanest, titled 'Zero Emission Vehicles', have to be available soon, since they are intended to make up 2 per cent of sales in 1997. Local authorities in London are campaigning to be allowed to enforce anti-pollution laws themselves; at present only the police have the power to do so, but they tend to be busy elsewhere. In Singapore, renting out road space to users is the way of the future.

C   When Britain's Royal Automobile Club monitored the exhausts of 60,000 vehicles, it found that 12 per cent of them produced more than half the total pollution. Older cars were the worst offenders; though a sizeable number of quite new cars were also identified as *gross polluters*, they were simply badly tuned. California has developed a scheme to get these gross polluters off the streets: they offer a flat $700 for any old, run-down vehicle driven in by its owner. The aim is to remove the heaviest-polluting, most decrepit vehicles from the roads.

D   As part of a European Union environmental programme, a London council is testing an infra-red spectrometer from the University of Denver in Colorado. It gauges the pollution from a passing vehicle – more useful than the annual stationary test that is the

British standard today – by bouncing a beam through the exhaust and measuring what gets blocked. The council's next step may be to link the system to a computerised video camera able to read number plates automatically.

E   The effort to clean up cars may do little to cut pollution if nothing is done about the tendency to drive them more. Los Angeles has some of the world's cleanest cars – far better than those of Europe – but the total number of miles those cars drive continues to grow. One solution is car-pooling, an arrangement in which a number of people who share the same destination share the use of one car. However, the average number of people in a car on the freeway in Los Angeles, which is 1.3, has been falling steadily. Increasing it would be an effective way of reducing emissions as well as easing congestion. The trouble is, Los Angelenos seem to like being alone in their cars.

F   Singapore has for a while had a scheme that forces drivers to buy a badge if they wish to visit a certain part of the city. Electronic innovations make possible increasing sophistication: rates can vary according to road conditions, time of day and so on. Singapore is advancing in this direction, with a city-wide network of transmitters to collect information and charge drivers as they pass certain points. Such road-pricing, however, can be controversial. When the local government in Cambridge, England, considered introducing Singaporean techniques, it faced vocal and ultimately successful opposition.

Part Two

The scope of the problem facing the world's cities is immense. In 1992, the United Nations Environmental Programme and the World Health Organisation (WHO) concluded that all of a sample of twenty megacities – places likely to have more than ten million inhabitants in the year 2000 – already exceeded the level the WHO deems healthy in at least one major pollutant. Two-thirds of them exceeded the guidelines for two, seven for three or more.

Of the six pollutants monitored by the WHO – carbon dioxide, nitrogen dioxide, ozone, sulphur dioxide, lead and particulate matter – it is this last category that is attracting the most attention from health researchers. PM10, a sub-category of particulate matter measuring ten-millionths of a metre across, has been implicated in thousands of deaths a year in Britain alone. Research being conducted in two counties of Southern California is reaching similarly disturbing conclusions concerning this little-understood pollutant.

A world-wide rise in allergies, particularly asthma, over the past four decades is now said to be linked with increased air pollution. The lungs and brains of children who grow up in polluted air offer further evidence of its destructive power. The old and ill, however, are the most vulnerable to the acute effects of heavily polluted stagnant air. It can actually hasten death, as it did in December 1991 when a cloud of exhaust fumes lingered over the city of London for over a week.

The United Nations has estimated that in the year 2000 there will be twenty-four megacities and a further eighty-five cities of more than three million people. The pressure on public officials, corporations and urban citizens to reverse established trends in air pollution is likely to grow in proportion with the growth of cities themselves. Progress is being made. The question, though, remains the same: 'Will change happen quickly enough?'

Questions 1–5

Look at the following solutions (Questions 1–5) and locations.

Match each solution with one location.

Write the appropriate locations in boxes 1–5 on your answer sheet.

NB You may use any location more than once.

SOLUTIONS

1   Manufacturers must sell cleaner cars.

2   Authorities want to have power to enforce anti-pollution laws.

3   Drivers will be charged according to the roads they use.

4   Moving vehicles will be monitored for their exhaust emissions.

5   Commuters are encouraged to share their vehicles with others.

LOCATIONS
Singapore
Tokyo
London
New York
Mexico City
Cambridge
Los Angeles

Questions 6–10

Do the following statements reflect the claims of the writer in Reading Passage 1?

In boxes 6–10 on your answer sheet write

> **YES**   *if the statement reflects the claims of the writer*
> **NO**   *if the statement contradicts the claims of the writer*
> **NOT GIVEN** *if it is impossible to say what the writer thinks about this*

6   According to British research, a mere twelve per cent of vehicles tested produced over fifty per cent of total pollution produced by the sample group.

7   It is currently possible to measure the pollution coming from individual vehicles whilst they are moving.

8   Residents of Los Angeles are now tending to reduce the yearly distances they travel by car.

9   Car-pooling has steadily become more popular in Los Angeles in recent years.

10   Charging drivers for entering certain parts of the city has been successfully done in Cambridge, England.

Questions 11–13

*Choose the appropriate letters **A–D** and write them in boxes 11–13 on your answer sheet.*

11   How many pollutants currently exceed WHO guidelines in all megacities studied?

     A   one
     B   two
     C   three
     D   seven

12   Which pollutant is currently the subject of urgent research?

     A   nitrogen dioxide
     B   ozone
     C   lead
     D   particulate matter

13   Which of the following groups of people are the most severely affected by intense air pollution?

     A   allergy sufferers
     B   children
     C   the old and ill
     D   asthma sufferers

READING PASSAGE 2

*You should spend about 20 minutes on **Questions 14–27** which are based on Reading Passage 2 below.*

VOTES FOR WOMEN

The suffragette movement, which campaigned for votes for women in the early twentieth century, is most commonly associated with the Pankhurst family and militant acts of varying degrees of violence. The Museum of London has drawn on its archive collection to convey a fresh picture with its exhibition

The Purple, White and Green: Suffragettes in London 1906–14.

The name is a reference to the colour scheme that the Women's Social and Political Union (WSPU) created to give the movement a uniform, nationwide image. By doing so, it became one of the first groups to project a corporate identity, and it is this advanced marketing strategy, along with the other organisational and commercial achievements of the WSPU, to which the exhibition is devoted.

Formed in 1903 by the political campaigner Mrs Emmeline Pankhurst and her daughters Christabel and Sylvia, the WSPU began an educated campaign to put women's suffrage on the political agenda. New Zealand, Australia and parts of the United States had already enfranchised women, and growing numbers of their British counterparts

wanted the same opportunity.

With their slogan 'Deeds not words', and the introduction of the colour scheme, the WSPU soon brought the movement the cohesion and focus it had previously lacked. Membership grew rapidly as women deserted the many other, less directed, groups and joined it. By 1906 the WSPU headquarters, called the Women's Press Shop, had been established in Charing Cross Road and in spite of limited communications (no radio or television, and minimal use of the telephone) the message had spread around the country, with members and branch officers stretching to as far away as Scotland.

The newspapers produced by the WSPU, first *Votes for Women* and later *The Suffragette*, played a vital role in this communication. Both were sold throughout the country and proved an invaluable way of informing members of meetings, marches, fund-raising events and the latest news and views on the movement.

Equally importantly for a rising political group, the newspaper returned a profit. This was partly because advertising space was bought in the paper by large department stores such as Selfridges, and jewellers such as Mappin & Webb. These two, together with other like-minded commercial enterprises sympathetic to the cause, had quickly identified a direct way to reach a huge market of women, many with money to spend.

The creation of the colour scheme provided another money-making opportunity which the WSPU was quick to exploit. The group began to sell playing cards, board games, Christmas and greeting cards, and countless other goods, all in the purple, white and green colours. In 1906 such merchandising of a corporate identity was a new marketing concept.

But the paper and merchandising activities alone did not provide sufficient funds for the WSPU to meet organisational costs, so numerous other fund-raising activities combined to fill the coffers of the 'war chest'. The most notable of these was the Woman's Exhibition, which took place in 1909 in a Knightsbridge ice-skating rink, and in 10 days raised the equivalent of £250,000 today.

The Museum of London's exhibition is largely visual, with a huge number of items on show. Against a quiet background hum of street sounds, copies of *The Suffragette*, campaign banners and photographs are all on display, together with one of Mrs Pankhurst's shoes and a number of purple, white and green trinkets.

Photographs depict vivid scenes of a suffragette's life: WSPU members on a self-proclaimed 'monster' march, wearing their official uniforms of a white frock decorated with purple, white and green accessories; women selling *The Suffragette* at street corners, or chalking up pavements with details of a forthcoming meeting.

Windows display postcards and greeting cards designed by women artists for the movement, and the quality of the artwork indicates the wealth of resources the WSPU could call on from its talented members.

Visitors can watch a short film made up of old newsreels and cinema material which clearly reveals the political mood of the day towards the suffragettes. The programme begins with a short film devised by the 'antis' – those opposed to women having the vote – depicting a suffragette as a fierce harridan bullying her poor, abused husband. Original newsreel footage shows the suffragette Emily Wilding Davison throwing herself under King George V's horse at a famous race-course.

Although the exhibition officially charts the years 1906 to 1914, graphic display boards outlining the bills of enfranchisement of 1918 and 1928, which gave the adult female populace of Britain the vote, show what was achieved. It demonstrates how advanced the suffragettes were in their thinking, in the marketing of their campaign, and in their work as shrewd and skilful image-builders. It also conveys a sense of the energy and ability the suffragettes brought to their fight for freedom and equality. And it illustrates the intelligence employed by women who were at that time deemed by several politicians to have 'brains too small to know how to vote'.

Questions 14 and 15

Choose the appropriate letters A–D and write them in boxes 14 and 15 on your answer sheet.

14　What is the main aspect of the suffragette movement's work to which the exhibition at the Museum of London is devoted?

    A　the role of the Pankhurst family in the suffrage movement
    B　the violence of the movement's political campaign
    C　the success of the movement's corporate image
    D　the movement's co-operation with suffrage groups overseas

15　Why was the WSPU more successful than other suffrage groups?

    A　Its leaders were much better educated.
    B　It received funding from movements abroad.
    C　It had access to new technology.
    D　It had a clear purpose and direction.

Question 16

*Choose **TWO** letters A–E and write them in box 16 on your answer sheet.*

In which **TWO** of the following years were laws passed allowing British women to vote?

    A　1906
    B　1909
    C　1914
    D　1918
    E　1928

Questions 17–19

Complete the notes below.

*Choose **NO MORE THAN THREE WORDS** from Reading Passage 2 for each answer.*

Write your answers in boxes 17–19 on your answer sheet.

> Three ways in which the WSPU raised money:
>
> • the newspapers: mainly through selling ...**17**...
> • merchandising activities: selling a large variety of goods produced in their ...**18**...
> • additional fund-raising activities: for example, ...**19**...

Questions 20–26

Do the following statements reflect the situation as described by the writer in Reading Passage 2?

In boxes 20–26 on your answer sheet write

    YES   *if the statement reflects the situation as described by the writer*
    NO   *if the statement contradicts the writer*
    NOT GIVEN *if it is impossible to know what the situation is from the passage*

Example	Answer
The WSPU was founded in 1906 by Emmeline Pankhurst.	**NO**

20   In 1903 women in Australia were still not allowed to vote.

21   The main organs of communication for the WSPU were its two newspapers.

22   The work of the WSPU was mainly confined to London and the south.

23   The WSPU's newspapers were mainly devoted to society news and gossip.

24   The Woman's Exhibition in 1909 met with great opposition from Parliament.

25   The Museum of London exhibition includes some of the goods sold by the movement.

26   The opponents of the suffragettes made films opposing the movement.

Question 27

Choose the appropriate letter A–D and write it in box 27 on your answer sheet.

The writer of the article finds the exhibition to be

    A   misleading.
    B   exceptional.
    C   disappointing.
    D   informative.

READING PASSAGE 3

*You should spend about 20 minutes on **Questions 28–40** which are based on Reading Passage 3 below.*

Measuring Organisational Performance

There is clear-cut evidence that, for a period of at least one year, supervision which increases the direct pressure for productivity can achieve significant increases in production. However, such short-term increases are obtained only at a substantial and serious cost to the organisation.

To what extent can a manager make an impressive earnings record over a short period of one to three years by exploiting the company's investment in the human organisation in his plant or division? To what extent will the quality of his organisation suffer if he does so? The following is a description of an important study conducted by the Institute for Social Research designed to answer these questions.

The study covered 500 clerical employees in four parallel divisions. Each division was organised in exactly the same way, used the same technology, did exactly the same kind of work, and had employees of comparable aptitudes.

Productivity in all four of the divisions depended on the number of clerks involved. The work entailed the processing of accounts and generating of invoices. Although the volume of work was considerable, the nature of the business was such that it could only be processed as it came along. Consequently, the only way in which productivity could be increased was to change the size of the work group.

The four divisions were assigned to two experimental programmes on a random basis. Each programme was assigned at random a division that had been historically high in productivity and a division that had been below average in productivity. No attempt was made to place a division in the programme that would best fit its habitual methods of supervision used by the manager, assistant managers, supervisors and assistant supervisors.

The experiment at the clerical level lasted for one year. Beforehand, several months were devoted to planning, and there was also a training period of approximately six months. Productivity was measured continuously and computed weekly throughout the year. The attitudes of employees and supervisory staff towards their work were measured just before and after the period.

Turning now to the heart of the study, in two divisions an attempt was made to change the supervision so that the decision levels were pushed *down* and detailed supervision of the workers reduced. More general supervision of the clerks and their supervisors was introduced. In addition, the managers, assistant managers, supervisors and assistant supervisors of these two divisions were trained in group methods of leadership, which they endeavoured to use as much as their skill would permit during the experimental year. For easy reference, the experimental changes in these two divisions will be labelled the 'participative programme'.

In the other two divisions, by contrast, the programme called for modifying the supervision so as to increase the closeness of supervision and move the decision levels *upwards*. This will be labelled the 'hierarchically controlled programme'. These changes were accomplished by a further extension of the scientific management approach. For example, one of the major changes made was to have the jobs timed and to have standard times computed. This showed that these divisions were overstaffed by about 30%. The general manager then ordered the managers of these two divisions to cut staff by 25%. This was done by transfers without replacing the persons who left; no one was to be dismissed.

Results of the Experiment

Changes in Productivity
Figure 1 shows the changes in salary costs per unit of work, which reflect the change in productivity that occurred in the divisions. As will be observed, the hierarchically controlled programmes increased productivity by about 25%. This was a result of the direct orders from the general manager to reduce staff by that amount. Direct pressure produced a substantial increase in production.

A significant increase in productivity of 20% was also achieved in the participative programme, but this was not as great an increase as in the hierarchically controlled programme. To bring about this improvement, the clerks themselves participated in the decision to reduce the size of the work group. (They were aware of course that productivity increases were sought by management in conducting these experiments.) Obviously, deciding to reduce the size of a work group by eliminating some of its members is probably one of the most difficult decisions for a work group to make. Yet the clerks made it. In fact, one division in the participative programme increased its productivity by about the same amount as each of the two divisions in the hierarchically controlled programme. The other participative division, which historically had been the poorest of all the divisions, did not do so well and increased productivity by only 15%.

Changes in Attitudes
Although both programmes had similar effects on productivity, they had significantly different results in other respects. The productivity increases in the hierarchically controlled programme were accompanied by shifts in an adverse direction in such factors as loyalty, attitudes, interest, and involvement in the work. But just the opposite was true in the participative programme.

For example, Figure 2 shows that when more general supervision and increased participation were provided, the employees' feeling of responsibility to see that the work got done increased. Again, when the supervisor was away, they kept on working. In the hierarchically controlled programme, however, the feeling of responsibility decreased, and when the supervisor was absent, work tended to stop.

As Figure 3 shows, the employees in the participative programme at the end of the year felt that their manager and assistant manager were 'closer to them' than at the beginning of the year. The opposite was true in the hierarchical programme. Moreover, as Figure 4 shows, employees in the participative programme felt that their supervisors were more likely to 'pull' for them, or for the company and them, and not be solely interested in the company, while in the hierarchically controlled programme, the opposite trend occurred.

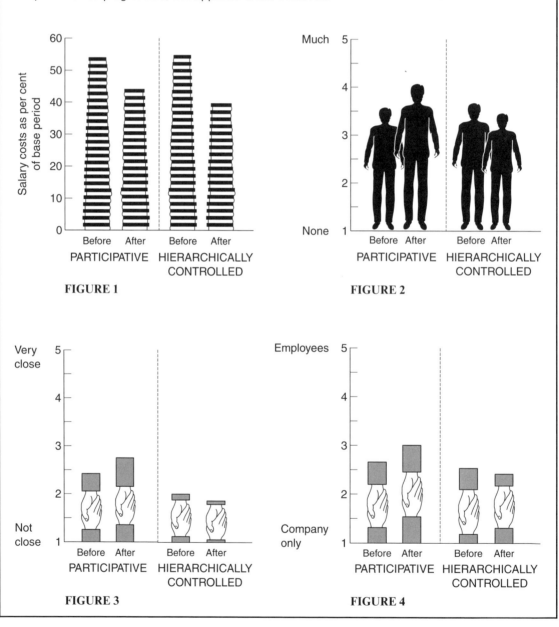

FIGURE 1

FIGURE 2

FIGURE 3

FIGURE 4

Questions 28–30

*Choose the appropriate letters **A–D** and write them in boxes 28–30 on your answer sheet.*

28 The experiment was designed to

   A establish whether increased productivity should be sought at any cost.
   B show that four divisions could use the same technology.
   C perfect a system for processing accounts.
   D exploit the human organisation of a company in order to increase profits.

29 The four divisions

   A each employed a staff of 500 clerks.
   B each had equal levels of productivity.
   C had identical patterns of organisation.
   D were randomly chosen for the experiment.

30 Before the experiment

   A the four divisions were carefully selected to suit a specific programme.
   B each division was told to reduce its level of productivity.
   C the staff involved spent a number of months preparing for the study.
   D the employees were questioned about their feelings towards the study.

Questions 31–36

*Complete the summary below. Choose **ONE** word from Reading Passage 3 for each answer.*

Write your answers in boxes 31–36 on your answer sheet.

This experiment involved an organisation comprising four divisions, which were divided into two programmes: the hierarchically controlled programme and the participative programme. For a period of one year a different method of . . . **31** . . . was used in each programme. Throughout this time . . . **32** . . . was calculated on a weekly basis. During the course of the experiment the following changes were made in an attempt to improve performance.

In the participative programme:

* supervision of all workers was . . . **33** . . .
* supervisory staff were given training in . . . **34** . . .

In the hierarchically controlled programme:

* supervision of all workers was increased.
* work groups were found to be . . . **35** . . . by 30%.
* the work force was . . . **36** . . . by 25%.

Questions 37–40

Look at Figures 1, 2, 3 and 4 in Reading Passage 3.

*Choose the most appropriate label, **A–I**, for each Figure from the box below.*

Write your answers in boxes 37–40 on your answer sheet.

A	Employees' interest in the company
B	Cost increases for the company
C	Changes in productivity
D	Employees' feelings of responsibility towards completion of work
E	Changes in productivity when supervisor was absent
F	Employees' opinion as to extent of personal support from management
G	Employees feel closer to their supervisors
H	Employees' feelings towards increased supervision
I	Supervisors' opinion as to closeness of work group

37 *Fig 1* ....

38 *Fig 2* ....

39 *Fig 3* ....

40 *Fig 4* ....

WRITING

WRITING TASK 1

You should spend about 20 minutes on this task.

> ***The graph below shows the unemployment rates in the US and Japan between March 1993 and March 1999.***
>
> ***Write a report for a university lecturer describing the information shown below.***

You should write at least 150 words.

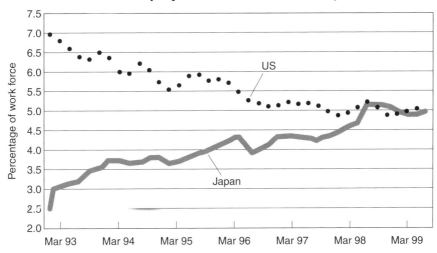

Unemployment Rates: US and Japan

WRITING TASK 2

You should spend about 40 minutes on this task.

Present a written argument or case to an educated reader with no specialist knowledge of the following topic.

> *Improvements in health, education and trade are essential for the development of poorer nations. However, the governments of richer nations should take more responsibility for helping the poorer nations in such areas.*
>
> *To what extent do you agree or disagree with this opinion?*

You should use your own ideas, knowledge and experience and support your arguments with examples and relevant evidence.

You should write at least 250 words.

SPEAKING

PART 1

The examiner asks the candidate about him/herself, his/her home, work or studies and other familiar topics.

EXAMPLE

Daily Routine

- What would you like to change in your daily routine?
- Are all your days the same?
- Tell me about your typical weekday and your typical weekend.
- What is the balance of work/study and free time in your normal day?

PART 2

> **Describe something you own which is very important to you.**
> **You should say:**
>   **where you got it from**
>   **how long you have had it**
>   **what you use it for**
> **and explain why it is so important to you.**

You will have to talk about the topic for 1 to 2 minutes. You have one minute to think about what you're going to say. You can make some notes to help you if you wish.

PART 3

Discussion topics:

How values can change

Example questions:
What kind of possessions show status in your country?
Do you think it was different for your grandparents?

The consumer society

Example questions:
Modern society is often called 'materialistic'. Why do you think this is?
Do you think consumerism is a positive or a negative development?

The consumer market

Example questions:
What is the role of advertising?
How do you think the Internet will affect buying patterns in the future?

General Training: Reading and Writing Test A

SECTION 1   *Questions 1–13*

Questions 1–8

Look at the advertisements opposite.

Write the appropriate letters A–E in boxes 1–8 on your answer sheet.

A	International Language Centre
B	Global Language Learning Centre
C	TAFE International
D	Club Français
E	University of Canberra

Which advertisement mentions

1   up-to-date teaching systems?

2   that the institution has been established for a significant time?

3   examination classes?

4   that arrangements can be made for activities outside class?

5   the availability of courses for school students?

6   language teaching for special purposes?

Which **TWO** advertisements mention

7   a wide variety of language choices?

8   evening classes?

A

INTERNATIONAL LANGUAGE CENTRE

INSTITUTE OF TECHNOLOGY

FRENCH & JAPANESE
SUMMER INTENSIVE

Also commencing January 1997

* Mandarin * Cantonese * Thai
* Vietnamese * Korean * Indonesian * English
* Spanish * Italian * German * Russian

For further details contact:

Admissions & Information Office
5 Bligh Street,
Sth. Sydney, 2000

Tel: 295 4561
Fax: 235 4714

B

Global Language Learning Centre

ONE OF THE WORLD'S BEST LANGUAGE SCHOOLS IS
NOW IN SYDNEY

LEARN A NEW LANGUAGE
IN 10–20 WEEKS

LATEST METHODS
DAY AND EVENING COURSES

BUSINESS, HOSPITALITY
OR TRAVEL
CHOICE OF 9 LANGUAGES

Phone for Appointment
938 0977

C

DO YOU WANT TO LEARN ENGLISH SOMEWHERE DIFFERENT?

Then come to Perth, the Picturesque Capital City of Western Australia

Situated on the beautiful Swan River, Perth offers you . . .

- Mediterranean climate
- lovely Indian Ocean beaches
- every sport imaginable
- multicultural society
- government owned TAFE Colleges
- high standards of facilities and staff
- maximum flexibility
- hostel or homestay accommodation

Intensive English Courses Available

- 5 intakes per year
- 10 week modules
- multicultural classes
- optional programs
- Cost: $2000 AUD per 10 weeks

Study Tours Available

- English/cultural/tourism

For further details, contact:

TAFE International,
Level 5, 1 Mill Street,
Perth 6000, Western Australia
Telephone: 619 320 3777

D

French
SUMMER COURSES
January 1997

Adults' Crash Course 9–19 Jan
Intensive 3 or 4 hrs a day,
morning or evening *30 hrs $250*
(Beginners and Low Intermediate only)

Adults' Normal Course 9 Jan–4 March
10 levels from Beginner to Advanced
Twice a week – 2 hrs morning or evening
Once a week, Saturday 9am–1.30pm *32hrs $278*

High School Crash Course 11–25 Jan
Intensive 3 hrs a day, 1pm–4pm
Years 8 to 12 *24hrs $200*
Starts Wednesday 11.1.97

Club Français
27 Claire St, Sydney, Phone 227 1746

E

 UNIVERSITY OF CANBERRA

Learn English in Australia's National Capital

*   The TESOL Centre has more than 24 years' experience in providing quality language programs for overseas students

*   Test preparation, possibility of further academic study

*   Access to University facilities

*   Classes conducted on campus with opportunity to mix with Australian students

Questions 9–13

Read the notice about road works below.

In boxes 9–13 on your answer sheet write

> **TRUE**   *if the statement is true*
> **FALSE**   *if the statement is false*
> **NOT GIVEN** *if the information is not given in the notice*

9   The road will be closed for two days and not re-opened until Monday.

10   The road will be open as far as Little Street.

11   Work on the road will continue each weekend for the next month.

12   Temporary traffic lights will operate at intersections with Main Street.

13   There will be bus services to the university throughout the weekend.

MAIN STREET, GATTON RE-DEVELOPMENT

ROAD WIDENING TO AFFECT WEEKEND TRAFFIC AND BUS SERVICES TO THE UNIVERSITY CAMPUS

The next stage in the re-development of the roads in the town of Gatton will mean that Main Street will be closed between Little and Denning Streets from 6am on Saturday, 12 August to 6pm on Sunday, 13 August. The intersections of these streets with Main Street will not be affected.

We expect that the work will be completed at this time without further disruption to traffic.

Motorists should note that Main Street will be closed over the weekend during the hours indicated.

No university bus services will operate through the area between Little and Denning Streets. However, alternative services will operate on bus routes 566 and 45 between Gatton Road, the town centre and the university.

The Transport and Roads Department apologises for any inconvenience caused while improvements are in progress.

SECTION 2 *Questions 14–26*

Questions 14–19

Read the enrolment details for Ashwood College on the following page and look at the statements below.

In boxes 14–19 on your answer sheet write

> **TRUE** *if the statement is true*
> **FALSE** *if the statement is false*
> **NOT GIVEN** *if the information is not given in the passage*

Example	Answer
Overseas students may enrol for a course at the college from their home country.	**TRUE**

14 Overseas students must pay a deposit when they apply for a course at the college.

15 Outstanding fees are payable by the end of the first week of the course.

16 Classes are organised according to ability level.

17 There is a break between each lesson.

18 Students may change courses at any time during the term.

19 Any student is permitted to take a week's holiday during a 12-week course.

ASHWOOD COLLEGE

How to enrol if you are abroad . . .

Please complete the Application Form and send this with the correct Non-Returnable Deposit (see below) to: The Overseas Registrar, Ashwood College, 20 Glossop Street, Midhaven.
Tel: 01423–968075; Fax: 01423–968076.

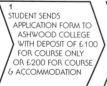

1
STUDENT SENDS APPLICATION FORM TO ASHWOOD COLLEGE WITH DEPOSIT OF £100 FOR COURSE ONLY OR £200 FOR COURSE & ACCOMMODATION

2
ASHWOOD COLLEGE CHECKS AVAILABILITY OF COURSE AND ACCOMMODATION

3
ASHWOOD COLLEGE SENDS STUDENT
— confirmation letter
— invoice
— certificate of enrolment
— transfer request form

4
STUDENT RETURNS COMPLETED AIRPORT TRANSFER FORM IF REQUIRED

8
STUDENT PAYS ANY OUTSTANDING BALANCE FOR COURSE AND ACCOMMODATION

7
STUDENT ARRIVES IN MIDHAVEN AND IS TESTED, INTERVIEWED AND PLACED IN CLASS

6
STUDENT CONFIRMS TIME OF ARRIVAL TO HOST FAMILY OR TO ASHWOOD COLLEGE

5
ASHWOOD COLLEGE CONFIRMS TRANSFER

How to enrol if you are in Midhaven . . .

We invite you to visit us and see the school. After an assessment you will be able to reserve a place on the next available course. We have two centres in Midhaven.

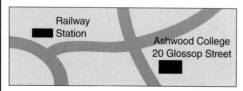

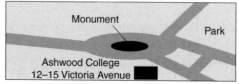

Deposits/payment

1. Your enrolment form must be accompanied by the course deposit of £100 or, if you are booking accommodation through the school, your course and accommodation deposit of £200.
2. Any balance of course and accommodation fees must be paid in full by the first day of your course.
3. All bank charges incurred in sending money to Ashwood College must be paid by the student.
4. Deposits and payments are non-refundable and non-transferable.
5. A charge of £20 will be made for any changes made to bookings.

Conditions

Timetable
Each hour consists of 50 minutes' tuition and a 10-minute break.

Public and School Holidays
There is no reduction in the fee where a course includes a Public Holiday, except for two weeks at Christmas.

Age
The above centres of Ashwood College do not accept students under 16 years of age.

Attendance
Students are expected to attend regularly and on time. Students forfeit tuition if they arrive late, are absent or leave before the course ends.

Student Holidays
Students on long courses except examination preparation courses may take a holiday of one week every 12 weeks without losing their course fee for this period.

Location and Time of Courses
Ashwood College has two all-year centres and a summer centre in Midhaven. Before entry to the school, students must take an entry test to determine the level of class they enter. We cannot guarantee the time or location of a student's course although every attempt is made to place students in the centre and at the time of their choice.

Questions 20–26

Read the information on the Language Institute on the following page.

Complete the summary of information below.

*Choose **NO MORE THAN THREE WORDS AND/OR NUMBERS** from the passage for each answer.*

Write your answers in boxes 20–26 on your answer sheet.

SUMMARY

Example	*Answer* **Totara Language Institute**
Overseas students who study at .... may choose to spend more of their free time	

with local students by applying for a room in the ...**20**... . Places are available here even for students enrolled on the minimum length course of ...**21**... . Class sizes for each course range from ...**22**... students and all the class teachers are well qualified; many of them teach on graduate programmes in areas such as applied linguistics. As a member of the Language Institute you will automatically be able to join the ...**23**... .

Hamilton can offer students a wide range of social activities. The city itself lies on either side of the ...**24**... which results in some very ...**25**... views and enjoyable walks in the gardens.

The Institute employs an activities co-ordinator who can help you organise your free time and you may also wish to make use of this service for planning your ...**26**... when you leave New Zealand. Remember that a student permit is not valid when you have finished your studies.

THE TOTARA LANGUAGE INSTITUTE NEW ZEALAND

Study English in a national university with students from many countries.

- **4-week blocks**
- **5 hours' tuition each day**
- **examination preparation**
- **university entry (with appropriate academic and English requirements)**

Choice of accommodation for all students – homestays with local families or in Halls of Residence with New Zealand students.

The Totara Language Institute is part of the University of Waikato in the city of Hamilton, in New Zealand's North Island. Intensive English classes are taught in four-week blocks throughout the year and students may enrol for as many blocks as they wish. Classes are for 5 hours each day, Monday to Friday, and include preparation for several international English language examinations. All the courses are taught by highly qualified teachers, many of whom also teach on Language Institute graduate programmes in second language teaching and applied linguistics. Classes are small, usually from 10–12 students with a maximum number of 15, and normally contain a mix of students from a wide range of countries. Students who study English at the Language Institute become international members of the Waikato Students' Union. The option is available to move on to university study if students meet the English language and academic entry levels for their choice of programme. The Language Institute provides student support, welfare and activities services. Students are met at Auckland airport on arrival and accommodation is provided with local families or in University Halls of Residence with New Zealand students.

Hamilton, one of New Zealand's fastest growing cities, is ideally located for a wide range of leisure and cultural activities. The Waikato river, the longest river in New Zealand, flows through the centre of the city, providing a picturesque and park-like setting of riverside walks and gardens. The Waikato region is a diverse agricultural area, rich in historic sites, arts and crafts, hot springs, native forests, mountains and rivers. Within easy reach is an unspoilt coastline; the wild and rugged west coast beaches famous for surfing, and the more peaceful east coast resorts are only a short drive from Hamilton. Further afield the mountains of the central North Island, 3 hours' drive away, provide superb ski facilities in winter, and hiking country in summer.

The Language Institute activities co-ordinator can assist students to arrange any sport and leisure activities. Assistance is also available for ongoing travel arrangements for students. Students on a visitor visa or work permit may study for a maximum of 3 months. Courses of longer duration require a student permit which is issued for the length of study only.

SECTION 3   *Questions 27–40*

Read the passage on the following pages.

Question 27

From the list below choose the most suitable title for the whole of the Reading Passage.

Write the appropriate letter A–D in box 27 on your answer sheet.

    A   Pollution control in coal mining
    B   The greenhouse effect
    C   The coal industry and the environment
    D   Sustainable population growth

Questions 28–31

The Reading Passage has four sections A–D.

Choose the most suitable heading for each section from the list of headings below.
Write the appropriate numbers i–viii in boxes 28–31 on your answer sheet.

List of Headings

  i   Global warming
  ii   The dangers of the coal industry
  iii   Superclean coal
  iv   Environment protection measures
  v   Coal as an energy source
  vi   Coal and the enhanced greenhouse effect
  vii Research and development
  viii Mining site drainage

---

28   Section **A**

29   Section **B**

30   Section **C**

31   Section **D**

A   Coal is expected to continue to account for almost 27 per cent of the world's energy needs. However, with growing international awareness of pressures on the environment and the need to achieve sustainable development of energy resources, the way in which the resource is extracted, transported and used is critical.

A wide range of pollution control devices and practices is in place at most modern mines and significant resources are spent on rehabilitating mined land. In addition, major research and development programmes are being devoted to lifting efficiencies and reducing emissions of greenhouse gases during coal consumption. Such measures are helping coal to maintain its status as a major supplier of the world's energy needs.

B   The coal industry has been targeted by its critics as a significant contributor to the greenhouse effect. However, the greenhouse effect is a natural phenomenon involving the increase in global surface temperature due to the presence of greenhouse gases – water vapour, carbon dioxide, tropospheric ozone, methane and nitrous oxide – in the atmosphere. Without the greenhouse effect, the earth's average surface temperature would be 33–35 degrees C lower, or –15 degrees C. Life on earth, as we know it today, would not be possible.

There is concern that this natural phenomenon is being altered by a greater build-up of gases from human activity, perhaps giving rise to additional warming and changes in the earth's climate. This additional build-up and its forecast outcome has been called the enhanced greenhouse effect. Considerable uncertainty exists, however, about the enhanced greenhouse effect, particularly in relation to the extent and timing of any future increases in global temperature.

Greenhouse gases arise from a wide range of sources and their increasing concentration is largely related to the compound effects of increased population, improved living standards and changes in lifestyle. From a current base of 5 billion, the United Nations predicts that the global population may stabilise in the twenty-first century between 8 and 14 billion, with more than 90 per cent of the projected increase taking place in the world's developing nations. The associated activities to support that growth, particularly to produce the required energy and food, will cause further increases in greenhouse gas emissions. The challenge, therefore, is to attain a sustainable balance between population, economic growth and the environment.

The major greenhouse gas emissions from human activities are carbon dioxide (CO_2), methane and nitrous oxide. Chlorofluorocarbons (CFCs) are the only major contributor to the greenhouse effect that does not occur naturally, coming from such sources as refrigeration, plastics and manufacture. Coal's total contribution to greenhouse gas emissions is thought to be about 18 per cent, with about half of this coming from electricity generation.

C   The world-wide coal industry allocates extensive resources to researching and developing new technologies and ways of capturing greenhouse gases. Efficiencies are likely to be improved dramatically, and hence CO_2 emissions reduced, through combustion and gasification techniques which are now at pilot and demonstration stages.

Clean coal is another avenue for improving fuel conversion efficiency. Investigations are under way into superclean coal (3–5 per cent ash) and ultraclean coal (less than 1 per cent ash). Superclean coal has the potential to enhance the combustion efficiency of conventional pulverised fuel power plants. Ultraclean coal will enable coal to be used in advanced power systems such as coal-fired gas turbines which, when operated in combined cycle, have the potential to achieve much greater efficiencies.

D   Defendants of mining point out that, environmentally, coal mining has two important factors in its favour. It makes only temporary use of the land and produces no toxic chemical wastes. By carefully pre-planning projects, implementing pollution control measures, monitoring the effects of mining and rehabilitating mined areas, the coal industry minimises the impact on the neighbouring community, the immediate environment and long-term land capability.

Dust levels are controlled by spraying roads and stockpiles, and water pollution is controlled by carefully separating clean water runoff from runoff which contains sediments or salt from mine workings. The latter is treated and re-used for dust suppression. Noise is controlled by modifying equipment and by using insulation and sound enclosures around machinery.

Since mining activities represent only a temporary use of the land, extensive rehabilitation measures are adopted to ensure that land capability after mining meets agreed and appropriate standards which, in some cases, are superior to the land's pre-mining condition. Where the mining is underground, the surface area can be simultaneously used for forests, cattle grazing and crop raising, or even reservoirs and urban development, with little or no disruption to the existing land use. In all cases, mining is subject to stringent controls and approvals processes.

In open-cut operations, however, the land is used exclusively for mining but land rehabilitation measures generally progress with the mine's development. As core samples are extracted to assess the quality and quantity of coal at a site, they are also analysed to assess the ability of the soil or subsoil material to support vegetation. Topsoils are stripped and stockpiled prior to mining for subsequent dispersal over rehabilitated areas. As mining ceases in one section of the open-cut, the disturbed area is reshaped. Drainage within and off the site is carefully designed to make the new land surface as stable as the local environment allows: often dams are built to protect the area from soil erosion and to serve as permanent sources of water. Based on the soil requirements, the land is suitably fertilised and revegetated.

Questions 32–36

*Choose the appropriate letters **A–D** and write them in boxes 32–36 on your answer sheet.*

32   The global increase in greenhouse gases has been attributed to

    A   industrial pollution in developing countries.
    B   coal mining and electricity generation.
    C   reduced rainfall in many parts of the world.
    D   trends in population and lifestyle.

33   The proportion of all greenhouse gases created by coal is approximately

    A   14 per cent.
    B   18 per cent.
    C   27 per cent.
    D   90 per cent.

34   Current research aims to increase the energy-producing efficiency of coal by

    A   burning it at a lower temperature.
    B   developing new gasification techniques.
    C   extracting CO_2 from it.
    D   recycling greenhouse gases.

35   Compared with ordinary coal, new, 'clean' coals may generate power

    A   more cleanly and more efficiently.
    B   more cleanly but less efficiently.
    C   more cleanly but at higher cost.
    D   more cleanly but much more slowly.

36   To control dust at mine sites, mining companies often use

    A   chemicals which may be toxic.
    B   topsoil taken from the site before mining.
    C   fresh water from nearby dams.
    D   runoff water containing sediments.

Questions 37–40

Do the following statements reflect the opinions of the writer in the Reading Passage?

In boxes 37- 40 on your answer sheet write

> **YES**   *if the statement reflects the opinion of the writer*
> **NO**   *if the statement contradicts the writer*
> **NOT GIVEN** *if it is impossible to say what the writer thinks about this*

37 The coal industry should be abandoned in favour of alternative energy sources because of the environmental damage it causes.

38 The greatest threats to the environment are the gases produced by industries which support the high standard of living of a growing world population.

39 World population in the twenty-first century will probably exceed 8 billion.

40 CFC emissions have been substantially reduced in recent years.

WRITING

WRITING TASK 1

You should spend about 20 minutes on this task.

> *You are due to start a new job next week but you will not be able to because you have some problems.*
>
> *Write a letter to your new employer. In your letter*
> * *explain your situation*
> * *describe your problems*
> * *tell him/her when you think you can start.*

You should write at least 150 words.

You do **NOT** need to write your own address.

Begin your letter as follows:

Dear ....,

WRITING TASK 2

You should spend about 40 minutes on this task.

You have been asked to write about the following topic.

> *Some people believe that children's leisure activities must be educational, otherwise they are a complete waste of time.*
>
> *Do you agree or disagree?*
>
> *Give reasons for your answer and include any relevant examples from your experience.*

You should write at least 250 words.

General Training: Reading and Writing Test B

SECTION 1   *Questions 1–13*

Questions 1–4

Read the information on The Medicine in the passage below.

Do the following statements agree with the information in the passage?

In boxes 1–4 on your answer sheet write

YES	*if the statement agrees with the information*
NO	*if the statement contradicts the information*
NOT GIVEN	*if there is no information about this in the passage*

Example	*Answer*
You must shake the bottle before you take the medicine	**YES**

1 You should lie down after you have taken the medicine.

2 You must stop taking the medicine if your eyesight is affected.

3 You must stop taking the medicine when you feel better.

4 This medicine is suitable for a person of any age.

The Medicine

- This medicine must be taken as directed.
- Before using, shake the bottle.
- Dose: 50ml to be taken twice daily after the midday and evening meals.

Instructions:

- Do not take this medicine on an empty stomach or immediately before lying down.
- If any of the following occur, discontinue taking the medicine and contact your doctor: dizziness, vomiting, blurred vision.
- This medicine is not available without a prescription and is not suitable for children under 5 years.
- Once you have begun to take this medicine you must continue to take it until the bottle is empty, unless advised otherwise by your doctor.
- Only one course of this medicine should be taken in a period of six months.
- Expiry date: 16 February, 2004

Questions 5–9

Look at the notice below.

Using ***NO MORE THAN THREE WORDS AND/OR A NUMBER*** *answer the following questions.*

Write your answers in boxes 5–9 on your answer sheet.

Example	*Answer*
What has been found in some Fancy Foods products?	**pieces of metal**

5   Where can you find the batch number on the jars?

6   How much will you receive for an opened jar of contaminated Chicken Curry?

7   If you have eaten Chicken Curry from a jar with one of the batch numbers listed, whom should you contact?

8   What information do they ask you to provide about the jar of Chicken Curry you ate?

9   What is the maximum reward Fancy Foods is offering for information about who contaminated their product?

IMPORTANT NOTICE: PRODUCT RETURN

Fancy Foods wishes to inform the public that pieces of metal have been found in some jars of Fancy Foods Chicken Curry (Spicy). The batches of the jars involved have numbers from J6617 to J6624. The batch number is printed on the bottom of each jar.

If you have any jars with these batch numbers, please return them (preferably unopened) to the supermarket where you purchased them. You can also return them to the factory (Fancy Foods Retailers, Blacktown). Fancy Foods will pay $10 for each jar returned unopened and $5 for each jar already opened.

No payment will be made for empty jars, which do not need to be returned. However, the company's Retailing Manager will be interested to hear from people who have consumed chicken curry from any of the above batch numbers. In particular, it will be helpful if they can give information about the place of purchase of the product.

Jars of Fancy Foods Chicken Curry (Coconut) and Fancy Foods Chicken Curry (Mango) have not been affected and do not need to be returned.

REWARD

Fancy Foods will pay a reward of $10,000 to $50,000 for information which leads to the conviction of any person found guilty of placing metal pieces in its products. If you have such information, please contact the Customer Relations Manager, Fancy Foods Retailers, Blacktown.

Questions 10–13

Look at the extract from a brochure on the following page.

*From the list of headings below, choose the most suitable headings for Sections **C–F**.*

*Write the appropriate numbers **i–viii** in boxes 10–13 on your answer sheet.*

Example	*Answer*
Section **A**	**viii**

10   Section **C**

11   Section **D**

12   Section **E**

13   Section **F**

List of Headings

i	Payment options
ii	Save money by not paying interest
iii	Choosing your style of furniture
iv	Free advice on furnishing your home
v	Location of stores
vi	Applying for a card
vii	Ordering furniture from home
viii	A wide range of furniture

FABULOUS FURNITURE

Section A

Have you ever wanted to buy a small bedside table? Or a dinner table for 20 people? If you want it, we've got it! Fabulous Furniture has Australia's widest choice of furniture.

Section B

If you visit a Fabulous Furniture store, you can have your furniture – right now – using our Fabulous Furniture Credit Card. When you see something you really want, you can have it straight away, and pay later.

Section C

Unlike most cards, the Fabulous Furniture Credit Card offers a full 60-day interest-free period on every Fabulous purchase – no matter when you make your purchase. This leaves you with more money to spend on other things.

Section D

- You may choose to pay the full amount within 60 days. In this case, you pay no interest.
- You may spread your payments over a longer period. In this case, interest will be charged after the initial 60-day interest-free period.

Section E

Application is absolutely free! Nor are there any annual fees or administration fees. Just fill in the application form and bring it to your nearest Fabulous Furniture store. Your application will be processed promptly and you can begin making purchases immediately after your application is approved.

Section F

We have stores in every major city, so you're never far away from a Fabulous Furniture store. For our addresses, just check in your local telephone directory.

SECTION 2   *Questions 14–27*

Questions 14–17

Read the notice on the following page about Student Clubs and Societies.

*The notice has four main paragraphs **A–D**.*

Choose the most suitable heading for each paragraph from the list of headings below.

*Write the appropriate numbers **i–x** in boxes 14–17 on your answer sheet.*

List of Headings
i   English Society
ii   Education Club
iii Film Appreciation Society
iv   Drama Society
v   Music Club
vi   Games Society
vii Women's Club
viii Debating Club
ix   United Nations Student Club
x   Technical Students' Club

14   Paragraph **A**

15   Paragraph **B**

16   Paragraph **C**

17   Paragraph **D**

Questions 18 and 19

*Using **NO MORE THAN THREE WORDS**, answer the following questions.*

Write your answers in boxes 18 and 19 on your answer sheet.

18   How do you let the CAS President know you are interested in joining a club?

19   How often is the CAS Ball held?

STUDENT CLUBS AND SOCIETIES

Desperate to find friends with common interests?
Urgently in need of student contacts around college?
Looking for different cultural and religious experiences?
Wanting some good discussion?

Don't look any further!

JOIN A CLUB OR SOCIETY AND HAVE FUN!

A ....

This club was first started by a group of friends who enjoyed going to the cinema. When our trips became more frequent we realised that there must be others who also shared our love of movies. This club is for those people. Membership gives wide access to other activities like basketball and football as well as barbecues and other social functions. We don't just enjoy movies.

B ....

The association has many opportunities to debate and we are a non-political unbiased international organisation which aims to promote international awareness on campus. We establish links and access to the organisation's agencies and other internationalist organisations and their resources. Our plans this year include discussion groups, guest speakers and to build a model of the UN General Assembly.

C ....

Whether for fun or debating experience, we discuss everything from personal experience, future society or feminism. This year we plan an internal competition, weekly debates and beginners' lessons as well as chances to compete nationally. Whether it be to improve your verbal or social skills the society provides both!

D ....

Want to be a movie star? Then go somewhere else! On the other hand, want to work really hard for great rewards? Then come and join the club where interesting theatre is created. We usually put on three productions each year. So if you like to write, paint, act, direct or do anything in the theatre, come and put your name down with us.

If you are interested in joining any of these clubs, you can leave a message for the President at the CAS Office in the Student Union Building.
And don't forget the CAS Ball is an annual event!
This year it's being held on 22 December!

Questions 20–27

It is possible for some students in Higher Education in Britain to borrow money through a government scheme. These loans are called 'student loans' and are described in the passage on the following page.

Read the passage and answer Questions 20–27 below.

In boxes 20–27 on your answer sheet write

YES   *if the answer to the question is 'yes'*
NO   *if the answer to the questions is 'no'*
NOT GIVEN *if the information is not given in the passage*

Example	*Answer*
I'm a full-time student at a local college of Higher Education. I already get a standard maintenance grant. Does this mean I'm not eligible for a student loan?	**NO**

20   I'm taking a month's cookery course at a local college. It's a private catering college. I'm going a couple of evenings a week, after work. I get a diploma at the end of it. Can I get some help with a student loan?

21   I'm starting a foundation course in September. It's full time and after a year I hope to get on to a degree course. The fees for the actual course are being paid for by my Local Authority. Am I eligible for a student loan?

22   I finish my first degree in July. I've got a place on a Postgraduate Certificate in Education course to start in September. Will the Local Authority pay the tuition fees for this course?

23   Now all her children are grown up my mother says she'd like to finish the studies she was forced to give up earlier in life. She's 48 now and her course is full-time for a year. Is she too old to get a student loan?

24   I've already been given a small scholarship to cover some of my tuition fees. Can I still get a student loan?

25   I'm actually staying with my aunt while I'm at college. Will the Student Loans Company want to know how much she earns?

26   I owed the bank rather a lot of money a few years ago. It's all paid back now but they won't lend me any more. Will this disqualify me from getting a student loan?

27   I took a course a couple of years ago, got a student loan, but had to withdraw half-way through. I've kept up all my payments on my loan. Am I eligible for a second loan?

Student Loans

The Government has been funding a loans scheme for students in Higher Education since September 1990.

These loans are available as a 'top up' to the standard grant. Although the loan is intended to supplement the grant for living costs, eligibility for a student loan is not restricted to those who receive a maintenance grant.

The decision whether or not to take the loan is yours.

Eligibility

You are eligible for a student loan if you are a UK resident and are attending a full-time Higher Education course, below postgraduate level, or a Postgraduate Certificate in Education course, provided you start your course before your 50th birthday. Full-time courses last at least one academic year and include sandwich courses which combine time at college with time spent in a workplace.

Eligible courses are offered by colleges, universities, the Scottish grant-aided colleges and other publicly funded institutions providing Higher Education courses.

In general, eligible courses include first degree courses or their equivalents and any other courses for which your Local Authority will pay your tuition fees.

Your financial circumstances

Students who want loans are not 'means tested' or 'credit vetted' – all those eligible will obtain a loan.

This means that:
- The amount of your maintenance grant or tuition fees does not matter.
- Other income, if any, is not taken into account.
- Any previous student loans are not taken into account.
- The income of your parents, spouse, partner or other relatives is not taken into account.
- Your previous financial record is not a consideration.

When to apply for a loan

If you would like more information on how to apply for a student loan in readiness for your entry to Higher Education in Autumn 2003, then you should contact The Student Loans Company from June 2003 onwards.

Once in Higher Education, you can apply for a loan at any time in the academic year.

SECTION 3　　*Questions 28–40*

Look at the passage below.

FIRST IMPRESSIONS COUNT

A　Traditionally uniforms were – and for some industries still are – manufactured to protect the worker. When they were first designed, it is also likely that all uniforms made symbolic sense – those for the military, for example, were originally intended to impress and even terrify the enemy; other uniforms denoted a hierarchy – chefs wore white because they worked with flour, but the main chef wore a black hat to show he supervised.

B　The last 30 years, however, have seen an increasing emphasis on their role in projecting the image of an organisation and in uniting the workforce into a homogeneous unit – particularly in 'customer facing' industries, and especially in financial services and retailing. From uniforms and workwear has emerged 'corporate clothing'. "The people you employ are your ambassadors," says Peter Griffin, managing director of a major retailer in the UK. "What they say, how they look, and how they behave is terribly important." The result is a new way of looking at corporate workwear. From being a simple means of identifying who is a member of staff, the uniform is emerging as a new channel of marketing communication.

C　Truly effective marketing through visual cues such as uniforms is a subtle art, however. Wittingly or unwittingly, how we look sends all sorts of powerful subliminal messages to other people. Dark colours give an aura of authority while lighter pastel shades suggest approachability. Certain dress style creates a sense of conservatism, others a sense of openness to new ideas. Neatness can suggest efficiency but, if it is overdone, it can spill over and indicate an obsession with power. "If the company is selling quality, then it must have quality uniforms. If it is selling style, its uniforms must be stylish. If it wants to appear innovative, everybody can't look exactly the same. Subliminally we see all these things," says Lynn Elvy, a director of image consultants *House of Colour*.

D　But translating corporate philosophies into the right mix of colour, style, degree of branding and uniformity can be a fraught process. And it is not always successful. According to *Company Clothing* magazine, there are 1000 companies supplying the workwear and corporate clothing market. Of these, 22 account for 85% of total sales – £380 million in 1994.

E　A successful uniform needs to balance two key sets of needs. On the one hand, no uniform will work if staff feel uncomfortable or ugly. Giving the wearers a choice has become a key element in the way corporate clothing is introduced and managed. On the other, it is pointless if the look doesn't express the business's marketing strategy. The greatest challenge in this respect is time. When it comes to human perceptions, first impressions count. Customers will size up the way staff look in just a few seconds, and that few seconds will colour their attitudes from then on. Those few seconds can be so important that big companies are prepared to invest years, and millions of pounds, getting them right.

F In addition, some uniform companies also offer rental services. "There will be an increasing specialisation in the marketplace," predicts Mr Blyth, Customer Services Manager of a large UK bank. The past two or three years have seen consolidation. Increasingly, the big suppliers are becoming 'managing agents', which means they offer a total service to put together the whole complex operation of a company's corporate clothing package – which includes reliable sourcing, managing the inventory, budget control and distribution to either central locations or to each staff member individually. Huge investments have been made in new systems, information technology and amassing quality assurance accreditations.

G Corporate clothing does have potential for further growth. Some banks have yet to introduce a full corporate look; police forces are researching a complete new look for the 21st century. And many employees now welcome a company wardrobe. A recent survey of staff found that 90 per cent welcomed having clothing which reflected the corporate identity.

Questions 28–33

The passage *First Impressions Count* has seven paragraphs **A–G**.

Which paragraphs discuss the following points?

*Write the appropriate letters **A–G** in boxes 28–33 on your answer sheet.*

Example	Answer
the number of companies supplying the corporate clothing market	**D**

28 different types of purchasing agreement

29 the original purposes of uniforms

30 the popularity rating of staff uniforms

31 involving employees in the selection of a uniform

32 the changing significance of company uniforms

33 perceptions of different types of dress

Questions 34–40

Do the following statements agree with the views of the writer of the passage?

In boxes 34–40 on your answer sheet write

> **YES** if the statement agrees with the writer's views
> **NO** if the statement contradicts the writer's views
> **NOT GIVEN** if it is impossible to say what the writer thinks about this

34 Uniforms were more carefully made in the past than they are today.

35 Uniforms make employees feel part of a team.

36 Using uniforms as a marketing tool requires great care.

37 Being too smart could have a negative impact on customers.

38 Most businesses that supply company clothing are successful.

39 Uniforms are best selected by marketing consultants.

40 Clothing companies are planning to offer financial services in the future.

WRITING

WRITING TASK 1

You should spend about 20 minutes on this task.

> *You are unhappy about a plan to make your local airport bigger and increase the number of flights. You live near the airport.*
>
> *Write a letter to your local newspaper. In your letter*
> * *explain where you live*
> * *describe the problem*
> * *give reasons why you do not want this development.*

You should write at least 150 words.

You do **NOT** need to write your own address.

Begin your letter as follows:

Dear Sir/Madam,

WRITING TASK 2

You should spend about 40 minutes on this task.

You have been asked to write about the following topic.

> **It is generally accepted that families are not as close as they used to be.**
>
> **Give some reasons why this change has happened and suggest how families could be brought closer together.**
>
> **Include any relevant examples from your experience.**

You should write at least 250 words.

TAPESCRIPTS

TEST 1

SECTION 1

JANICE:	Hello . . . Flagstone.
JON:	Oh hello; is that Flagstone Properties?
JANICE:	Yes that's right. *Flagstone here.* How can I help you? *Example*
JON:	Hello. I'm ringing just to make enquiries about renting a house. My name's Jon Anderson.
JANICE:	Yes, Mr Anderson. What sort of thing were you looking for?
JON:	Two-bedroomed house with garden.
JANICE:	Well . . . yes, sir, that shouldn't be any problem . . . just to let you know that our main areas, *the main areas we deal with, are the city centre itself* . . . *Q1*
JON:	City centre . . . uh-huh.
JANICE:	And the north suburbs.
JON:	Oh well . . . we were most interested in the Northern areas actually.
JANICE:	Right . . . yes . . . What sort of price were you thinking of?
JON:	Well . . . could you give me some idea?
JANICE:	Certainly. It really ranges from £250 per month. *Q2*
JON:	Only £250?
JANICE:	Yes, to about £500 depending on a number of different factors.
JON:	What does it depend on?
JANICE:	Well, obviously the quality of the area. And then whether there's a garden. *Q3*
JON:	Well, as I said, we'd want a garden.
JANICE:	And a garage pushes up the price.
JON:	Right . . . well, we wouldn't necessarily need one. I think about £350 a month would be our limit.
JANICE:	OK. Well . . . would you like to have a look at a couple of properties, sir?
JON:	Yes, that'd be great.
JANICE:	Looking at our files . . . I think we've got two which might suit you . . .
JON:	Hang on. I'll just get a pen. Right.
JANICE:	OK. Well, there's one on West Park Road which is £325 a month. *Q4*
JON:	Are the bills included?
JANICE:	Well, that one just includes the water bill. *Q5*
JON:	OK, right.
JANICE:	And the second house is in Tithe Road. I'll just spell that for you . . . OK?
JON:	Yep.
JANICE:	T-I-T-H-E Road.
JON:	Got that. And how much is that one?
JANICE:	That's £380.

JON:	380. Is that including water?	
JANICE:	No, I'm afraid not, <u>but it does include the telephone rental.</u>	*Q6*
JON:	Oh well, that's not too bad then. So, . . .	

- -

JANICE:	So, when would you be available to see them?	
JON:	Well, I'll be in town next week . . . say . . . Thursday?	
JANICE:	No, I'm sorry we don't have any availability for Thursday. <u>How about Wednesday afternoon?</u>	*Q7*
JON:	OK. That's fine. Would 5.00 be OK?	
JANICE:	Yes, fine. 5.00 it is. Just come to the Flagstone Offices.	
JON:	Oh, before I forget. What sort of things do I need to get done . . . to rent with you?	
JANICE:	Well, the most important thing is a letter from your bank . . .	
JON:	No problem . . .	
JANICE:	And then <u>a reference letter from your employer.</u>	*Q8*
JON:	Yes, that's OK.	
JANICE:	Great, and then <u>we would need you to give 2 weeks' notice of moving in . . .</u>	*Q9*
JON:	Right . . . 2 weeks' notice. And <u>what about a deposit?</u>	*Q10*
JANICE:	<u>That's one month's rent,</u> whatever the amount is.	
JON:	OK. One month. Is that it?	
JANICE:	No, sorry, one more . . . you will have to pay for the contract.	
JON:	Oh yes. I'd forgotten about that. OK, fine. So I'll start arranging those, and I'll . . .	
JANICE:	. . . I'll see you next week.	
JON:	Yes. Thanks very much. Bye.	
JANICE:	Goodbye.	

SECTION 2

MRS SMITH:	Hello, Mrs Sutton. Come in. How are you settling in next door? Have all your things from Canada arrived yet? I thought I saw a removals van outside your house yesterday afternoon.
MRS SUTTON:	Yes. They came yesterday. We spent all day yesterday arranging them. It's beginning to feel a bit more like home now.
MRS SMITH:	That's good. Look, come in and sit down. Are you alright? You look a bit worried.
MRS SUTTON:	Well, I am a bit. I'm sorry to bother you so early, Mrs Smith, but I wonder if you could help me. Could you tell me how I can get hold of a doctor? <u>Our daughter, Anna, isn't very well this morning</u> and I may have to call somebody out. <u>She keeps being sick and I am beginning to get a bit worried.</u> I just don't know how the health system works here in England. All I know is that it's very different from ours back in Canada.
MRS SMITH:	Well, I don't know really where to start. Let me think. Well, the first thing you have to do is find a family doctor – sometimes we call them general

Q11 appears to the right of the Mrs Sutton paragraph.

practitioners as well – and register with him or her. If you live here, you've got to be on a doctor's list. If you're not, things can be a bit difficult. Nobody will come out to you if you're not registered. Anyway, they work in things called practices. Sort of small groups of family doctors all working together in the same building. Now what you've got to do this morning is register with one of them.

Q12

There are two practices near here, so we're quite well off for doctors in this part of Manchester. There's the Dean End Health Centre about ten minutes' walk away and there's another practice in South Hay. That's about five minutes away going towards the town centre. We're registered at the Dean End one, but they're both OK. There are about six doctors in our practice and four in the other. So ours is quite big in comparison. And the building and everything's a bit more modern. South Hay is a bit old-fashioned but the doctors are OK. Their only problem is that they don't have a proper appointment system. Sometimes you have to wait for ages there to see someone.

Q13
Q14

Q15

Anyway, you go to the receptionist in whichever health centre and ask her to register you with a doctor there. You have to fill in a form, but it doesn't take long. Ours is called Dr Jones and we've been going to him for years – ever since we moved here fifteen years ago. I wouldn't say he's brilliant but I suppose he's alright really. We're used to him now. They say he's very good with elderly people, but he does tend to get a bit impatient with children. Listen, the one who's supposed to be really good with small children is Dr Shaw. I've heard lots of people say that. She's young and she's got small children of her own. So you could try registering with her. And if her list is full, I heard somebody say the other day that there's a really nice young doctor at South Hay, a Dr Williams. He holds special clinics for people with back trouble. But that's not really your problem, is it?

Q16

Q17

MRS SMITH: If you want a doctor to visit you at home, you have to ask for a home visit. You're supposed to do that before 10.30 in the morning, but obviously, if it's an emergency, you can phone at any time, night or day. It might not be your doctor that comes, though. It's quite often one of the other doctors in the practice. It doesn't really seem to make much difference.

Otherwise you make an appointment to see your doctor at the health centre. You usually get seen the same day. Not always of course, but usually, as I say. They hold surgeries between 9 and 11.30 every weekday, and from 4 to 6.30 Monday to Thursday. Saturdays are only for emergencies.

Q18

When the doctor sees you, he gives you a prescription. He writes what medication you need on it and you take it to a chemist's shop. There's one opposite the centre.

If it's for a child under 16, you don't have to pay. So if it's for Anna, there's no problem. The same thing goes if you're unemployed or retired, or if you're pregnant. Just as well because it's not cheap. You pay the same

Q19

price for each item the doctor has prescribed. <u>At the moment it's</u>   *Q20*
<u>something like £5 per item</u>. So you pay for the medication but the
consultation with the doctor doesn't cost you anything. It's completely free
as long as you're a resident here. You're going to be here for three years,
aren't you? So there shouldn't be any question of you paying anything to
see the doctor. So that's one less problem to worry about.

    Look, Mrs Sutton. If you want, I'll sit with your daughter for half an
hour if you want to go down to the health centre to register. It's no trouble
really, don't worry.

MRS SUTTON: Are you sure you wouldn't mind? That would really help me a lot. I'll ask
them if they can send someone round later to see Anna. I think I'll try the
Dean End Centre.

MRS SMITH: Good idea. Don't worry about Anna.

MRS SUTTON: Right. I'll be back as soon as I can.

SECTION 3

TUTOR: Hello. Jonathan Briggs, isn't it?

JB: Yes, that's right.

TUTOR: Do come in and sit down.

JB: Thanks.

TUTOR: Right. Well, Jonathan, as we explained in your letter, in this part of the
interview we like to talk through your application form . . . your experience to
date, etc. . . . and then in the second part you go for a group interview.

JB: Group interview . . . yes, I understand . . .

TUTOR: So . . . your first degree was in Economics?

JB: Yes, but <u>I also did Politics as a major strand</u>.   *Q21*

TUTOR: And you graduated in 1989. And I see you have been doing some teaching . . .

JB: Yes. <u>I worked as a volunteer teacher in West Africa</u>. <u>I was there for almost three</u>   *Q22*
<u>years</u> in total from 1990 to . . . umm . . . <u>1992</u>.   *Q23*

TUTOR: How interesting. What organisation was that with?

JB: It's not one of the major ones. <u>It's called Teach South</u>.   *Q24*

TUTOR: Oh, right. Yes, I have heard of it. It operates in several African countries,
doesn't it? And what kind of school was it?

JB: <u>A rural co-operative</u>.   *Q25*

TUTOR: Oh, a rural co-operative, how interesting . . . and what did you teach?

JB: A variety of things in different years . . . ummm . . . I did . . . <u>with Forms 1 to 3</u>   *Q26*
<u>mainly Geography</u> and <u>some English with Form 5</u>. Then in my final year I took   *Q27*
on some Agricultural Science with the top year . . . that's Form 6.

TUTOR: Right. Quite a variety then . . .

JB: I also ran the school farm.

TUTOR: How interesting . . .

TUTOR: . . . And how did you find the whole experience?

JB:	I'll be honest with you. At the end of the first year I really wanted to leave and come home.
TUTOR:	Why was that?
JB:	Well . . . I was very homesick at first and missed my family . . .
TUTOR:	Umm . . . I can quite understand that.
JB:	. . . and I also found it frustrating to have so few teaching resources, but I did decide to stay and in the end I extended my tour to a third year.
TUTOR:	Right. Things must have looked up then?
JB:	Yes. We set up a very successful project breeding cattle to sell locally.
TUTOR:	Really?
JB:	And then after a lot of hard work we finally got funds for new farm buildings.
TUTOR:	And you wanted to see things through?
JB:	Uh-huh.
TUTOR:	And is that why you want to train to teach Geography?
JB:	Yes. I've had a couple of jobs since then but I now realise I like teaching best. And I chose Geography because . . . because it is my favourite subject . . . and also because I think it has so many useful applications.
TUTOR:	Well . . . you certainly have had some interesting work experience. I'll ask you now to go on to the next stage of . . .

Q28 (beside "Well . . . I was very homesick at first and missed my family")

Q29 (beside "And I chose Geography because . . . because it is my favourite subject")

Q30 (beside "also because I think it has so many useful applications")

SECTION 4

ANNOUNCER:	Today's Health Counsel is presented by Paula Clayburg, who is the chief Counsellor at Liverpool's famous pain clinic: The Wilton Clinic. Paula . . .
PAULA CLAYBURG:	Do you know what Prince Charles, Seve Ballesteros and Elizabeth Taylor have in common? They all suffer from chronic back pain. In fact, bad backs are one of the most common health problems today, affecting people in all walks of life. The most recent available figures show that about a quarter of a million people are incapacitated with back pain every day.

Q31 (beside "about a quarter of a million people are incapacitated with back pain every day")

And many sufferers don't know the cause or the solution to their problem.

The majority of our patients at the clinic tend to be women. They are especially vulnerable because of pregnancy but also because of osteoporosis, which I personally believe to be the major cause of problems for women. I have many women patients who say they have completely given up exercise because the pain makes them so miserable. But of course that starts up a vicious circle. Bed rest, giving up exercise and pain killers are traditional responses to back pain but, although there are many excellent drugs on the market, at our clinic we are beginning to realise the unique benefits of relaxation therapy. Other specialists in the field make a strong case for certain types of exercise, but in our experience they are easily mishandled and can lead to more harm than good.

Q32 (beside "osteoporosis, which I personally believe to be the major cause of problems for women")

Q33 (beside "at our clinic we are beginning to realise the unique benefits of relaxation therapy")

Now, let's look at some of the reasons why back pain is developing into such a unique menace. In general, the body is pretty good at self-repair. A strain or a blow to a limb, though painful at the time, generally resolves itself. But the body's response to back injury can be very counter-productive. When pain strikes, we attempt to keep the back as immobile as possible, which makes the muscles tense up. Research shows that they often go into spasm, which causes further twisting of the spine. A vicious circle is underway.

Q34

The second mistake we often make when stricken with extreme back pain is to go to bed and stay there. Although at the clinic we recognise that a short rest in bed can be helpful . . . up to two days . . . any longer makes our back muscles become weaker and unable to hold up our spine. The pain therefore becomes worse.

Q35

Another problem is being overweight. Anyone a stone or more over-weight who already has back pain is not doing himself any favours: though it won't actually set it off in the first place, the weight will increase the strain and make things worse. The British diet could be partially to blame for the increase in back pain: over the last ten years the average weight of men has risen by 11 lbs and of women by 9 lbs. So much for the causes and aggravations of pain. But what can WE do to help?

Q36

There are many ways in which simple day-to-day care can make all the difference. The first point to watch of course is weight. If you are overweight, a diet will make all the difference.

Also, studies have shown that just one hour sitting in a slouched position can strain ligaments in the back which can take months to heal. At the clinic we have come to the conclusion that the major cause of the problem is not with the design of chairs, as some have suggested, but in the way WE sit in them. It can be useful to get special orthopaedic chairs, but remember the most important improvement should be in OUR posture.

Q37

Another enemy of your back is, of course, your beds. If your bed doesn't give enough support, back muscles and ligaments work all night trying to correct spinal alignment, so you wake up with a tired aching back. Try out an orthopaedic mattress or a spring slatted bed. Research shows that both can be beneficial for certain types of back pain.

Another hazard for your back are the shock waves which travel up your spine when you walk, known as heel strike. A real find for our patients has been the shock-absorbing shoe insert. A cheap but very effective solution. And you might be better off avoiding shoes with heels higher than 1½ inches. Though absolutely flat shoes can be a solution for some, others find their posture suffers.

Q38

Q39

Finally a word about the state-of-the-art relief – the TENS machine – a small battery-powered gadget which delivers subliminal electrical pulses to the skin. Our experience indicates that your money is better spent on the more old-fashioned remedies.

Q40

TEST 2

SECTION 1

RECEPTIONIST:	Sorry to keep you waiting. Well, firstly, let me give you this booklet. It tells you a bit more about the school, the courses and the social activities we offer. Now, on the first page, there's an outline of this morning's activities. There, you see? The programme starts at 10 o'clock. Try not to be late as it's a very full day.

<table>
<tr><td></td><td></td><td>Example</td></tr>
</table>

	At 10 o'clock, all the new students will gather in the Main Hall to meet the Principal and the rest of the staff. In fact, you spend most of the morning in the Main Hall.	*Q1*
STUDENT:	Where's that?	
RECEPTIONIST:	I'll show you in a minute. Just let me quickly run through this morning's events first and then I'll explain how to get there.	
STUDENT:	Yes, OK.	
RECEPTIONIST:	Right. Where were we? Yes, so, the Principal's talk will last about fifteen minutes and then the Director of Studies will talk to you for half an hour about the courses and the different requirements for each. After that, the Student Adviser will tell you about the various services and activities we offer to students. Any questions?	*Q2* *Q3*
STUDENT:	So, all of this is in the Main Hall?	
RECEPTIONIST:	That's right. And then you'll go next door to Classroom 5 at 11 o'clock.	*Q4*
STUDENT:	What happens there?	
RECEPTIONIST:	You'll have a test.	
STUDENT:	Test? I don't like the sound of that. What sort of test?	
RECEPTIONIST:	Oh, it's nothing to worry about. It's just a placement test to help us find your level of English so that we can put you in the right class. It won't last long.	*Q5*

- -

STUDENT:	But how do I find the Main Hall?	
RECEPTIONIST:	Right; if you look on the back of the booklet I gave you, you'll see a map of the school. Let me show you. Look; you came in through the Main Entrance, here, and now we're here at Reception. Now, to get to the Main Hall, you walk on to the end of this corridor in front of you and then you turn left. Walk along past the Language Laboratory and then past the Library, which is next to the Language Lab. on the same side, and facing you is the Main Hall, at the end of the corridor. You can't miss it.	*Q6*
STUDENT:	So it's next to the Library, in fact.	*Q7*
RECEPTIONIST:	Yes, that's right.	
STUDENT:	I should be able to find that. And do you have a Computer Laboratory?	
RECEPTIONIST:	Yes, we do.	

STUDENT:	Could you tell me where that is?	
RECEPTIONIST:	Certainly, yes. You go down to the end of this corridor again but, this time, don't turn left; turn right, away from the Main Hall. The Computer Lab. is immediately on your right. OK?	*Q8*
STUDENT:	And where's the staff room, in case I need to find a teacher at some stage?	
RECEPTIONIST:	The staff room is near the main entrance, on the left over there, just opposite the Reception desk. In a day or two, I'm sure you'll find your way around very easily.	*Q9*
STUDENT:	Oh, one last thing. Is there a student common room?	
RECEPTIONIST:	Oh yes, I forgot to mention that. It's this area here, very close to where we are now, to the right of the Reception desk as you come in the main entrance. There's tea and coffee facilities there.	*Q10*
STUDENT:	Great. Thank you very much.	
RECEPTIONIST:	You're welcome.	

SECTION 2

Hello, everybody and welcome to this informal meeting about the University Helpline. The Helpline was set up ten years ago by the Students Union and it aims to provide new students to the university with a service that they can use if they need information about practical areas of student life that they are unfamiliar with.

Let me give you some examples of the type of help we can offer. We can provide information on financial matters; for example, you may feel that your grant is insufficient to see you through college life or you may have some queries regarding the fees you are *Q11* paying if you are an overseas student. In both cases, the Helpline would be able to go through things with you and see what the outcome might be. Another area we can help *Q12* with is what we generally term the 'domestic' area; things such as childcare and the availability of nursery provision, for example, come under this. Then there's 'academic' issues that may arise while you are in the early stages of your course that you may not know what to do about. You may wish to know more about essay deadlines, for example, *Q13* or how to use the library – there are all kinds of questions you will find yourself asking and not knowing where to get quick answers from. The Helpline would be able to provide these. The last example I've given here is simply termed 'social' – and yes, there is a lot of *Q14* social life here! But you may have a particular interest you wish to pursue or you may wish *Q15* to participate in outings or trips if you don't know many people at the moment.

Let me give you some details so that you know where to go and who to see if you want to pay us a visit. Generally you will see our Helpline officer Jackie Kouachi, that's K-O-U-A- *Q16* C-H-I. Jackie is a full-time employee of the Student Union and she works in the Student Welfare Office – that's the office that deals with all matters related to student welfare and it's located at 13 Marshall Road. I have some maps here for those of you who haven't been there yet. If you wish to ring the office, the number is 326 99 40. That's 3269940. The *Q17* office is open between 9.30 and 6.00 on weekdays and from 10 to 4 on Saturdays and *Q18*

there'll be somebody there – usually Jackie or myself – between those times. If you want to
make an appointment you can phone or call at the office in person. Please note that it may *Q19*
not be possible for anyone to see you straight away – particularly if it is a busy time –
lunch time for example – and you may have to go on the waiting list and then come back *Q20*
later.

Well, enough from me. Any questions?

SECTION 3

TUTOR:	Good morning. So, we've looked at various aspects of staff selection this term and I think by now you should all be beginning to see how much more there is to it than just putting applicants through a short interview or asking the 'right' questions. So I think you should be ready for today's tutorial on 'matching the person to the job'.

We're going to talk today about the importance of choosing that all round *Q21*
'right' person.

MURIEL: Right. So we have to put ourselves into the role of the manager or supervisor?

TUTOR: Yes. And then we're going to imagine how different applicants would fit into the team or group they have to work with . . . er . . . we'll look at some examples later.

MURIEL: It's just theoretical at the moment . . .

TUTOR: Yes. The point is, you can select someone – even a friend – who has all the right
qualifications . . . degrees . . . certificates, whatever. You can also check that they
have a lot of experience . . . that they've done the sort of tasks that you want
them to do in your office already, in a similar environment. But if they start *Q22*
work and you realise that they just don't get along with everybody else, that . . .
say, they've got sharply contrasting views on how something will work . . . well,
with the best will in the world, you may be backing a loser.

DAVE: Wouldn't it be just a question of company training, though?

TUTOR: Not always. Particularly in a team situation, and I think it's important to think
in terms of that type of working environment. People have to have faith in each *Q23*
other's ability to carry out the task their boss has set them. They have to trust
that everyone will do their part of the job, and you can't necessarily train people
for this.

DAVE: But it's like trying to find out what someone's personality is like in a job
interview . . . I mean you just can't do that. Even if you try, you won't find out
what they're really like until they actually start work.

TUTOR: Well, in most interviews you usually ask candidates questions about their *Q24*
hobbies and what they like doing in their spare time . . . that sort of thing . . . so
employers are already involved in the practice of . . . well, doing part of the task.

DAVE: But it doesn't tell you anything. It doesn't tell you if they're easy-going or hate
smokers or whatever.

TUTOR: Well, arguably it does give you a bit of information about an applicant's
character.

TUTOR: Well, arguably it does give you a bit of information about an applicant's character, but also . . . more and more employers around the world are making use of what are called 'personality questionnaires' to help them select new staff and . . .

MURIEL: What's it called?

TUTOR: A Personality Questionnaire. They have to be filled out by the candidates some *Q25* time during the selection procedure, often just before an interview. The idea is actually quite old. Apparently they were used by the ancient Chinese for picking *Q26* out clerks and civil servants, and then later they were used by the military to *Q27* put people in appropriate areas of work. They've gained a lot of ground since then and there are about 80,000 different tests available now and almost two *Q28* thirds of the large employers use them.

MURIEL: Which makes you think that there must be something in them.

TUTOR: That's right. They ask the sort of questions that you might expect, like do you like working under pressure or are you good at keeping deadlines.

DAVE: And what if people can see through them and just write what they think the employer wants to see?

MURIEL: Well that's always a possibility.

DAVE: I mean, it's human nature to lie, isn't it?

TUTOR: Well, that's the point. Apparently it isn't. These tests are compiled by experts *Q29* and they believe that the answers can provide a few simple indicators as to roughly the type of person that you are . . . that people will generally be truthful in that situation.

MURIEL: And then you can go some way towards finding out whether someone's say, forward-looking . . . a go-ahead type of person . . . or resistant to change.

TUTOR: Yes. And there are all kinds of *(fade out)*

SECTION 4

TUTOR: Right. Are we all here? OK. As you know, today Vivien is going to do a *Example* presentation on the hat-making project she did with her class during her last teaching practice. So, over to you, Vivien.

VIVIEN: Thanks. Um . . . Mr Yardley has asked me to describe to you the project I did as a student teacher at a secondary school in London. I was at this school for six *Q31* weeks and I taught a variety of subjects to a class of fourteen-year-old pupils. *Q32* The project I chose to do was a hat-making project and I think this project could easily be adapted to suit any age. So, to explain the project . . .

After we'd done the research, we went back to the classroom to make two basic hat shapes using rolls of old wallpaper. We each made, first of all, a conical hat by . . . er . . . if I show you now . . . cutting out a circle and then *Q33* making one cut up to the centre and then . . . er . . . overlapping the cut like this this . . . a conical hat that sits on your head. The other hat we made was a little more complicated . . . er . . . first of all we cut out a circle again . . . like this . . . then you need a long piece with flaps on it – I've already made that bit which I

have here – you bend the flaps over and stick them . . . with glue or prittstick . . .   *Q34*
to the underside of the circle . . . like this. Again, I've prepared this so that I
don't get glue everywhere. The pupils do, of course, so you need plenty of covers
for the table. And there you have a pillbox hat as in *pill* and *box*. Now variations
and combinations of these two hat shapes formed the basis of the pupils' final
designs.

The next stage of the project was the design phase and this involved, first of all,   *Q35*
using their pages of research to draw a design of their hat on paper. That's the
easy part. They then had to translate their two-dimensional design into a form
to fit their head. I encouraged them to make a small-scale, three-dimensional   *Q36*
hat first so that they could experiment with how to achieve the form they
required and I imposed certain constraints on them to keep things simple. For
example, they had to use paper not card. Paper is more pliable and easier to
handle. They also had to limit their colours to white, grey or brown shades of   *Q37*
paper which reflected the colours of the buildings they were using as a model
for their hats and they had to make sure their glue didn't show!
     Well, it was very enjoyable and just to give you an idea of what they
produced, I've brought along three hats to show you. This one here is based on   *Q38*
a circular stairway in an old building in London. It uses three pillbox hats one
on top of the other. This was designed by Theresa. Here's another one that has   *Q39*
a simple strip going round the base of the hat but has then gone on to add strips
of paper that come out from the base and that meet at the top of the hat –
rather like a crown – making a fairly tall hat. This was made by Muriel. And
lastly there's a combination of the pillbox or single strip around the base and   *Q40*
then the conical hat shape on top to form a castle turret. This was made by
Fabrice, and there are many more that I could have brought.
TUTOR: Thank you, Vivien. That was most interesting. Now what we can learn from this
     is that . . .

TEST 3

SECTION 1

JOAN: Right . . . let's try and get it sorted out today so we don't have it hanging over us. OK?

PETER: Good idea. I'll take notes.

JOAN: First thing . . . numbers . . . have we got anything definite?

PETER: Well . . . I've been working it out and I think 40 to 43.

JOAN: Shall we put 45 to be on the safe side?   *Example*

PETER: Yep, fine.

JOAN: Dates . . . well. That's straightforward.

PETER: The last working day before Christmas . . . which is . . .

JOAN: . . . which is December the 21st.

PETER: . . . which is going to be pretty difficult to book at Christmas so we'd better think of two or three places just to be on the safe side.

JOAN: Well, last year's was hopeless.

PETER: The Red Lion, wasn't it?

JOAN: Yep. We ought to go for something more expensive, cos you . . .

PETER: . . . you gets what you pay for.

JOAN: That new Indian restaurant in Wetherfield is supposed to be excellent . . . the   *Q1*
Rajdoot.

PETER: How do you spell that?

JOAN: R-A-J-D-O-O-T.

PETER: But it's bound to be packed.

JOAN: Well, let's put that down as the first choice and have some back-ups. What about
the Park View Hotel as a second choice?   *Q2*

PETER: Yes, that's always reliable. Park View Hotel . . .

JOAN: And the London Arms in case.   *Q3*

PETER: London Arms . . .

JOAN: I'll call them now if you want.

PETER: No. I'll do it, Joan. You're really busy. Have you got the numbers?

JOAN: Not for the Rajdoot, but . . . right . . . Park View Hotel: 777192 and . . .
London Arms: 208657.   *Q4*

PETER: Great. Before I ring, we'd better just make sure they're within the price range.

JOAN: Up to £15 a head?

PETER: I think you'll find some people won't be able to go that high.

JOAN: Well, you can't get anything decent under £10.

PETER: OK. We'll say £12?

JOAN: OK.

PETER: And we'd better make sure there's good vegetarian food.

JOAN: And a non-smoking section! You know what the boss is like.   *Q5*

PETER: Don't remind me. I'll let you know as soon as I get anything.

PETER:	Good news. I found Rajdoot's number straight away and they can fit us in. Their Christmas menu sounds great.	
JOAN:	What is it?	
PETER:	French onion soup or fruit juice.	
JOAN:	Uh-huh.	
PETER:	Roast dinner or <u>lentil curry</u> . . . sounds ordinary but my friend said it was really tasty.	*Q6*
JOAN:	Umm . . . lentil curry . . . that's unusual.	
PETER:	Then for dessert there's traditional plum pudding or apple pie, plus coffee.	
JOAN:	That sounds really good for £12. Did you book it?	
PETER:	Well, I said I'd check with the staff first. But they did say they'd hold the booking until next Wednesday anyway. Oh, and if we go ahead, <u>they'd like a £50 deposit</u>.	*Q7*
JOAN:	50 is normal . . . that's fine.	
PETER:	And they want a letter.	
JOAN:	Right . . . to confirm.	
PETER:	And they say with such large numbers <u>we have to choose the menu in advance</u>.	*Q8*
JOAN:	That won't be a problem. I'll put up a notice with details of the restaurant and the menu. When did you say they wanted confirmation by?	
PETER:	It was . . . let's see . . . <u>the 4th of November</u>.	*Q9*
JOAN:	Where do you think I should put up the notice? Where everyone's guaranteed to see it.	
PETER:	On the café noticeboard I should think.	
JOAN:	Hardly anyone looks at that.	
PETER:	Well, <u>the Newsletter is probably your best bet</u>.	*Q10*
JOAN:	Good idea. I'll go and do that now.	

SECTION 2

TUTOR:	. . . So, I'll hand over now to Julie Brooks.	
JULIE BROOKS:	Thank you. Welcome to the Sports Centre. It's good to see that there are so many people wanting to find out about our sports facilities.	
	First of all, membership. All students at the college are entitled to become members of the Sports Centre, <u>for an annual fee of £9.50</u>. To register with us and get your membership card, <u>you need to come to reception</u>, between 2 and 6 pm, Monday to Thursday. I'm afraid we can't register new members on Friday, so it's Monday to Thursday, 2 to 6, at reception. Now, there are three things that you must remember to bring with you when you come to register; they are: your Union card, a recent passport-sized photograph of yourself, and the fee. It doesn't matter whether you bring cash or a cheque. We can't issue your card unless you bring all three; so, don't forget: your Union card, passport photo and fee.	*Q11/Q12* *Q13*
	Then <u>once you have got your sports card, you will need to bring it with you whenever you come to book or use any Sports Centre facilities</u>.	*Q14/Q15*

Booking over the phone is not allowed, so you have to come here in person, with your card, when you want to book. Our opening hours seem to get longer every year. We are now open from 9am to 10pm on weekdays and from 10am to 6pm on Saturdays. *Q16*

For those of you who are up and about early in the morning, we are introducing a 50 per cent 'morning discount' this year. This is because the facilities tended to be under-used in the mornings last year. It means that all the sessions will be half-price between 9am and 12 noon on weekdays.

So, what exactly are the facilities? What sports can you play here? Well, this room we are in at the moment is called the Main Hall, and it's used mainly for team sports such as football, volleyball and basketball, but also for badminton and aerobics. On the other side of the reception area there is the dance studio; this provides a smaller, more intimate space, *Q17/Q18* which we use for ballet, modern dance and martial arts – not at the same time, of course. Then in a separate building, which you may have noticed on your way here . . . it's on the other side of the car park . . . there are *Q19/Q20* the squash courts (six of them), and at the far end of the building a fitness room. This is our newest facility, only completed in the Spring, but it is already proving to be one of the most popular. As well as all these facilities available here on the campus, we also have an arrangement with the local tennis club, which is only two miles away, entitling our students to use their courts on weekday mornings in the Summer.

So, I think that there should be something here for everybody, and I hope to see all of you at the Centre, making use of the facilities. If, in the course of the year, you have any suggestions as to how the service we provide might be improved or its appeal widened, I'll be interested to hear from you.

SECTION 3

JOHN BROWN:	Good morning, Mrs Collins. I just wondered if you could help me with this entry form for the Young Electronic Engineer competition.
MARY COLLINS:	Hello, John. Oh you've made the jigsaw for blind children, with the bleeper.
JOHN BROWN:	When they put a piece in correctly, that's right.
MARY COLLINS:	OK, let's have a look at the form.
JOHN BROWN:	Right, thanks. I've never filled in one of these before, so . . .
MARY COLLINS:	Well, let's just do it in pencil first. So, name of designers . . .
JOHN BROWN:	Well, Ann helped me with some of the electronics work.
MARY COLLINS:	Then you must put her name in as well. Right . . . Ann Ray.
JOHN BROWN:	Sorry. It's ANNE and her surname is spelt R-E-A.

Q21
MARY COLLINS:	Good start! OK . . . REA. And age is easy. You're both 16. What have you called the design? Keep it short.
JOHN BROWN:	What about jigsaw puzzle design for visually handicapped?
MARY COLLINS:	Too long. Just say blind puzzle, that'll do.

Q22

Q23

JOHN BROWN:	OK.
MARY COLLINS:	Right now, size of equipment?
JOHN BROWN:	I've got it noted down here . . . um, yes, length, sorry, width is 20 cm.
MARY COLLINS:	OK.
JOHN BROWN:	Length is 50 cm, and then the depth is . . . well, it's very little.
MARY COLLINS:	What would you say? I think you can be approximate.
JOHN BROWN:	I'd say 2.5 cm.
MARY COLLINS:	And the electricity supply? Is it mains operated?
JOHN BROWN:	No it isn't, it's actually battery.
MARY COLLINS:	OK, write battery.
JOHN BROWN:	Fine, OK. It's the next bit that I'm really not sure what to put.
MARY COLLINS:	Well, special features means, what is really new about this, you know, suitable for the group you made it for.
JOHN BROWN:	Well, it's safe for children.
MARY COLLINS:	That's fine. Put that in.
JOHN BROWN:	OK, and of course we think it's educational.
MARY COLLINS:	There you are, you've done it. Anything else?
JOHN BROWN:	Well, I think the price is good.
MARY COLLINS:	That's probably the most important factor.
JOHN BROWN:	OK . . . cheap price.
MARY COLLINS:	Which brings us on to the next bit. What's the cost?
JOHN BROWN:	Well, the pieces we made out of old wood . . . they cost, ooh, $5.
MARY COLLINS:	And the electrics?
JOHN BROWN:	They were more expensive . . . say, $9.50. Brilliant. Now what do they mean by other comments?
MARY COLLINS:	It's just a chance for you to say anything about the equipment, and problems you envisage.
JOHN BROWN:	Well, we would really like help with making plastic instead of wooden pieces.
MARY COLLINS:	Well, put something like, need help to make plastic pieces.
JOHN BROWN:	OK. And the other thing is, we'd like to develop a range of sizes.
MARY COLLINS:	That's fine, then, just put that. And the last bit is, when will you send the equipment?
JOHN BROWN:	Well, we've got a lot of work on at the moment and we want to get it as good as we can.
MARY COLLINS:	Well, say 25 June?
JOHN BROWN:	Can't we make it later?
MARY COLLINS:	Well, the last date is 1 July. Why not say that?
JOHN BROWN:	OK, that's what I'll put.
MARY COLLINS:	So that's the lot!
JOHN BROWN:	That's brilliant. Thanks very much, Mrs Collins. I'll send it off straightaway.
MARY COLLINS:	Glad to be of help. Very best of luck to you both.
JOHN BROWN:	Thanks, bye.
MARY COLLINS:	Bye.

Q24

Q25

Q26

Q27

Q28

Q29

Q30

SECTION 4

PAULA: Today I'd like to introduce Ted Hunter, who used to rear sheep and poultry but who is here to tell us about a rather unusual type of livestock that he's been concentrating on in the last few years. Ted Hunter is a member of the Domesticated Ostrich Farming Association, and is here to tell us about the possibilities of breeding and rearing these birds here in this country.

TED: Thank you, Paula. When you look at international restaurant menus and supermarkets they all tend to feature the same range of meats – beef, lamb, chicken, pork, that sort of thing. But people are always interested in something different and we're now finding that farming can bring new types of meat to our tables. The kangaroo is one animal that's now being farmed for its meat and eaten outside Australia, where it comes from. It looks and tastes rather like rabbit, though it's slightly darker in colour, but it is rather tough, so that's a problem for some people. Crocodiles are also being farmed for their meat. This is rather like chicken, pale and tender, and it's getting quite fashionable. Some people also find it's rather fatty, but I think it makes a really tasty sandwich. Now a third type of meat becoming increasingly available, and the one that I think is by far the nicest of the three, is ostrich, which most people say has a similar taste and texture to beef. However, it's much better for you than beef, as we'll see later.

    Most people think of ostriches as wild animals, but in fact ostriches have been farmed in South Africa since around 1860. At first they were produced for their feathers. In Africa they were used for tribal ceremonial dress and they were also exported to Europe and America where they were made into ladies' fans and used for decorating hats. Later, feather fans and big, decorated hats went out of fashion but ostriches were still bred, this time for their hide. This can be treated to produce about half a square metre of leather – very delicate, fine stuff of very good quality.

    At the same time, some of the meat was used for biltong – the air-dried strips of meat popular in South Africa as a sort of fast food.

    However, recently there's been more and more interest in the development of ostrich farming in other parts of the world, and more people are recognising its value as a food source. Ostrich meat is slightly higher in protein than beef – and much lower in fats and cholesterol. It tastes good too. A series of European taste tests found that 82% of people prefer ostrich to beef. And one ostrich produces a lot of meat – from around 30 to 50 kg, mostly from the hindquarters of the bird.

    Farmed ostriches don't need African climates, and in fact ostrich farming is now becoming well established in other parts of the world. However, setting up an ostrich farm isn't something to embark on lightly. Mature breeding birds are very expensive – even a fertilised ostrich egg isn't cheap so you need quite a bit of capital to begin with. Then the farmer needs special equipment such as incubators for the eggs. The young chicks are very dependent on human minders, and need a lot of attention from the people looking after them. In addition, ostriches can't be intensively farmed – they need space and exercise.

Q31

Q32

Q33

Q34

Q35

Q36

Q37

Q38

Q39

But in spite of this they make good farming sense. A cow produces only one calf a year whereas a female ostrich can lay an egg every other day. And because the farmers can use incubators and hatched chicks are nourished well and protected from danger, the failure rate on farms is very low indeed and almost all the fertilised eggs will hatch out into chicks which will in turn reach maturity. This is very different from the situation in the wild, where the vast majority of chicks will die or be killed before they grow up into mature ostriches. So it's possible, once the initial outlay has been made, for the farmer to be looking at very good profit margins indeed.

Q40

Ostrich farming is still in its early days outside Africa but we hope that ostrich meat will be freely available soon and before long will be as cheap as beef.

TEST 4

SECTION 1

SARAH:	John, I've just had some good news. Susan has had her baby.	
JOHN:	Do you know when she had it?	
SARAH:	Yesterday. The tenth of August.	*Example*
JOHN:	Oh, my father was born on August the tenth. Give me the details and I'll make a note for everyone at work.	
SARAH:	OK.	
JOHN:	Well, was it a boy or a girl?	
SARAH:	It's a boy.	
JOHN:	And what are they going to call him?	
SARAH:	Tom. Tom Lightfoot. It sounds quite good, don't you think?	
JOHN:	Yes, that has quite a good ring to it.	
SARAH:	You know he's quite a big baby. He weighed four and a quarter kilos when he was born.	*Q1*
JOHN:	That does sound big, four and a quarter kilos.	
SARAH:	And he's long too, forty-six centimetres.	*Q2*
JOHN:	Mmmm. Tall parents. He'll grow up to be over two metres, I'd say.	
SARAH:	With masses of black hair, curly black hair. You know, we should go and visit them in hospital. What about tomorrow afternoon at around 1pm?	
JOHN:	Yes, OK.	
SARAH:	Where should we meet? . . . Ah, I could come and pick you up at your house, if you like.	
JOHN:	Yes, that would be wonderful. My car is still off the road.	
SARAH:	Just refresh my memory. What's the address again?	
JOHN:	It's 15 Chesterfield Road, Paddington.	
SARAH:	It's next to the library, isn't it?	
JOHN:	Not exactly. It's next to a bank. The State Bank actually. The library is opposite us, on the corner.	*Q3/Q4*
SARAH:	That's right, and there's a garage on the other street corner. I remember now.	*Q5*
JOHN:	So, you'll pick me up at a quarter to one and we'll be there at one easily.	

SARAH:	Now what should we take? We must take them something.	
JOHN:	I always think flowers are good to take to someone in hospital, don't you?	
SARAH:	Well, not really. Everyone always brings flowers and they don't last. I think it's much better to take a pot plant, so she can take it home with her.	
JOHN:	Yes, but then she has to remember to water it. What about a big box of chocolates?	
SARAH:	OK, chocolates sound fine. We should get something for the baby too. What do you think?	*Q6*
JOHN:	Yes, you're right. What do you think of something like baby shampoo or talcum powder?	

SARAH: Or we could get a little hat, or something like that.

JOHN: We don't know the size, or the right colour, do we?

SARAH: I think we should get something they wouldn't normally buy. What about a soft toy of some sort?

JOHN: Yes, a soft toy.   *Q7*

SARAH: What about a teddy bear?

JOHN: I could get one early tomorrow at the market and I could probably get the   *Q8/Q9*
chocolates there too.

SARAH: Good.

JOHN: So you'll pick me up at a quarter to one at my place and I'll make sure that I've got the presents.

SARAH: You must remember how much you paid for the gifts, so I can pay you back for half. If they're going to be from both of us, I would like to go shares.

JOHN: OK. I'd say the chocolates would be about $15 for something nice and not too small and the toy would be around $35 or so, I'd think.   *Q10*

SARAH: Good, that'll be fine. About $25 each then. Good, I'll pick you up then on Sunday at twelve forty-five.

JOHN: OK.

SARAH: See you then. Bye.

SECTION 2

PRESENTER: Good evening. Tonight's show comes to you from the Good Home Exhibition in Duke's Court, where we've been trying out some of the latest gadgets on show here and getting our resident expert – Liz Shearer – to tell us which ones are worth buying and which will die a death.

LIZ SHEARER: Well, hello. Yes, John, I've been investigating four new household gadgets and sorting out the advantages and disadvantages and then really deciding what are 'Must buys', what are 'Maybe buys' and what are 'Never buys' Let's start with this vacuum flask for keeping drinks hot. Well . . . I felt this had quite a lot going for it, most of all is the fact that it contains no glass and is therefore unbreakable to all intents and purposes. It's made   *Q11*
of stainless steel which is guaranteed for 20 years . . . hope that's long enough . . . and it's true what the manufacturer claims – that it does   *Q12*
maintain heat for 18 hours. So that's pretty good. On the down side, it really works out to be quite expensive and, much more surprisingly, it   *Q13*
unfortunately leaves a strange taste . . . you know when you've drunk from it . . . so all in all, my recommendation would be it's got plenty of advantages, but it is rather expensive so I'd say you should maybe buy it.

Moving on to a natty little device . . . the Whistle Key Holder. Basically this is where you whistle and the key holder gives off a high pitched noise and flashes light so you can find it. One advantage of this model is that it also has a small light. You press the button and this means you can find keyholes easily. I also felt the small size was a real advantage. On the   *Q14* weaker side, I did find the noise unpleasant. Which I'm sure the designers could have done something about. And I found that it didn't work *Q15* through metal, so it's mainly useful for finding in coat pockets, cushions, etc. But taken as a whole I thought it was a masterpiece of design and *Q16* would highly recommend it.

The third gizmo is called the Army Flashlight because it was developed initially for military use. It works by squeezing the handle to generate the power. Its advantages are that it can be used for outside activities, and *Q17* also . . . and this is one of the surprising features . . . it does work underwater. My main objection to it though was although it did work in *Q18* these conditions, this model gave off a weak light. So my recommendation *Q19* I'm afraid would have to be to avoid this one.

The decoy camera was last on my list. This is a fake video camera which you fix to your wall to scare off burglars. The advantage of this model is something which makes it look very realistic . . . its flashing light. On the *Q20* down side, it was quite difficult to fix to the wall. However, burglary is such a major problem these days that it is worth the effort, so this gets my strong recommendation.

PRESENTER: OK. Thanks for that, Liz.

SECTION 3

BRYSON: Well, Amina, thanks for letting me have your draft in such good time.

AMINA: Oh, that's alright. I was just very anxious to hear what you think of it. You can see that I decided to change the topic – I had been interested in looking at Barings Factory.

BRYSON: Oh, I think the hospital was a much better choice. In fact . . . well . . . I have to *Q21* say that I thought it was good.

AMINA: Oh?

BRYSON: There's still lots of work to be done . . .

AMINA: Oh yes . . . of course.

BRYSON: But there's plenty of good ideas. It opens well and the first chapter is fine but the middle section really stood out for me . . . most interesting. *Q22*

AMINA: That's amazing because I really didn't find it a bit easy to write . . . *Q23*

BRYSON: How long did you work on the whole thing?

AMINA: Well, I spent about two or three weeks reading and doing general research and then I dashed the writing off very quickly . . . so about four weeks in all.

BRYSON: Well, that's about par for the course. You've got a while yet to make the changes.

AMINA: Oh right . . . no problem . . .

BRYSON: Right. Let's have a look at my notes here. OK. Starting with section headings . . . the broad divisions are good but you'll have to re-do the actual headings. *Example* I've made some suggestions in the margins . . .

AMINA: OK. Thanks.

| BRYSON: | Now, this information on local housing . . . I can see why you put it there but it really isn't relevant to the approach you've taken. | *Q24* |

BRYSON: Now, this information on local housing . . . I can see why you put it there but it really isn't relevant to the approach you've taken.   *Q24*

AMINA: I think I see what you mean.

BRYSON: Now . . . what did I say about the interviews?

AMINA: I worked very hard on those. I really thought they were valuable.

BRYSON: They are, Amina, but they're very complex and rather unclear at the moment. You're going to have to spend a bit of time making the data a lot clearer.   *Q25*

AMINA: OK . . . as long as I don't have to remove them altogether . . .

BRYSON: No, don't worry.

AMINA: What about the chronology . . . the list of dates? I wasn't sure whether I should rewrite those.

BRYSON: My advice on that is to take them out. I feel it makes the whole piece appear too simplistic.   *Q26*

AMINA: OK, if it'll help.

BRYSON: Now, there are a couple of other books I'd like you to look at. Have you got a pen? Right . . . *Approaches to Local History* by John Mervis . . .

AMINA: Right . . .

BRYSON: And then I think you need to think about ways of representing interview data. Have a look at *Sight and Sound* by Kate Oakwell.   *Q27*

AMINA: *Sight and Sound.*

BRYSON: Then you know I'm going away on holiday next week . . .

AMINA: Yes.

BRYSON: So when you've made the changes I suggest you show the work to your Support Tutor.   *Q28*

AMINA: Support Tutor . . . right . . .

BRYSON: Then you do the proof reading . . .   *Q29*

AMINA: Proof reading . . . uh-huh. When by, do you think?

BRYSON: I'd aim for 29 June and after that you should get it laser printed . . . but be careful because the computer centre closes on 10 July.   *Q30*

AMINA: And then I hand it in to . . . ?

BRYSON: Oh, the Faculty Office as usual.

AMINA: OK, that's fine. I think I'm all set now! Thanks very much for all your help.

BRYSON: A pleasure. See you when I get back.

AMINA: Yep. Thanks, Dr Bryson. Bye.

BRYSON: Bye.

SECTION 4

Good afternoon. I'm Paula Bundell and I am giving you the lectures on Environmental Noise this term. Today we are going to look into the effects of noise on a planned housing estate in a particularly difficult part of the new Manchester Park area.

This site is not as bad as some I have researched in the past. The Blacktown airport is closed from 6pm to 7am and this is a great advantage to the site. The only noise after dark

is from the highway and the traffic is somewhat reduced between 7.30pm and 5.30am. *Q31*
So, the people most affected by the noise will be, I expect, housewives. By the time most of *Q32*
the students and workers have arrived back home in the evening during the week the noise
will have abated to a fairly large extent. The weekends are still a problem of course, but the
traffic is certainly reduced on Saturdays to a large extent and even more so on Sundays. *Q33*

Of course modifications to houses will be necessary at a site like this and they come at a
significant cost to the developer and home buyer. The modifications I am about to outline
will add about $25,000 to the price of a newly-built house. That will still mean a cheaper *Q34*
house than in a less noisy and more desirable area.

A bit of background would not go astray. I understand that you are all familiar with the
proposed development site at Manchester Park.

It's a particularly difficult one in terms of noise with the highway along the eastern
perimeter and the Blacktown airport not 3 kilometres away to the north.

Of course, those nearest the highway will be the worst hit, with heavy traffic noise as
well as the noise from the light planes overhead. As you all know, the normal noise
threshold for private housing is 55 decibels. At this site the levels have been recorded as *Q35*
high as 67 decibels.

The construction of the houses has to be somewhat modified from houses in most areas. In
the houses on the highway and in the noisiest areas of this site there will be a need for
specialised double glazing and special acoustic seals will have to be fitted to the doors. *Example*
All exterior doors in this especially noisy pocket will have to be solid core wood doors with
hinges. Every house built on this site, not just those adjacent to the highway or nearest to
the airport, will require high density insulation materials in the roof. Not only will all the
roofs need insulating, the exterior walls will be required to be double brick. All ceilings will *Q36*
require double thickness plaster board to be used in the construction. In the noisiest areas
mechanical ventilation will have to be installed in the exterior walls. In those areas with *Q37*
sealed windows it will be necessary to fit fans with absorbers to cut out the noise in those
particular houses. Air conditioning units could also be fitted in the ceilings of such houses *Q38*
but this is substantially more expensive than fans, and may not be needed on this site.

Coming back now to the double glazing I mentioned before. Specialised double glazing
requires a larger air gap between the inner and outer glass than normal double glazing.
The gap must be at least 7 centimetres. The thickness of the glass is also a factor, 8 *Q39*
millimetres on the outside and 6 on the inside pane. It is essential that the glass be thicker
on the outside than on the inside and that the gap between the panes of glass be a
minimum of 7 centimetres.

Obviously, the noise factor will have to be taken into consideration with the layout of
the houses. Living areas will have to be designed at the back of the houses away from the
highway. Bedrooms and living rooms will have to be built towards the back, and for those *Q40*
houses closest to the highway two layers of plasterboard will be needed for the interior
bedroom walls. Those rooms constructed at the front of the houses should be garages,
laundries, kitchens, bathrooms and dining rooms.

I have come to the conclusion that this development should go ahead, but with various
acoustic modifications according to the position of the block in relation to the highway
and intersection.

Answer key

LISTENING

Each question correctly answered scores 1 mark. Please note! **CORRECT SPELLING NEEDED IN ALL ANSWERS.** *(Where alternative spellings are accepted these are stated in the key.)*

Section 1, Questions 1–10

1 (the) city centre (itself) *ACCEPT* center
2 (£) 250 (pounds) (to) (£) (about) 500 (pounds)
3 (a) garden
4 (£) 325 (pounds)
5 (the) water (bill(s))
6 (the) telephone/phone (rental)
7 Wednesday/Wed (afternoon)
8 (your) employer
9 two/2 weeks'/wks' // (a) fortnight's//fourteen/14 days'
10 (1/one) month('s) rent
   NOT one month

Section 2, Questions 11–20

11 (her) daughter (Anna) // Anna // Ana // (her) child
12 (a) practice // practices
13 (about) 6 // six (doctors)
14 (about) 4 // four (doctors)
15 better // more efficient // faster
16 elderly // old // older
17 back problems/trouble // bad backs
18 9 // nine (am) // 9.00 // nine/9 o'clock
19 *EITHER ORDER*
   B // unemployed people
   E // pregnant women
20 (£) 5 // five (pounds)

Section 3, Questions 21–30

21 Politics
22 (West) Africa
23 1990 to 1992
   NOT 1993
24 Teach South
25 rural co(-)operative
26 Geography
27 (Form) 5/five/V
28 (very) homesick // missed (my/his) family // homesickness
29 favourite subject *ACCEPT* favorite
30 (many) (useful) applications

Section 4, Questions 31–40

31 A
32 B // osteoporosis
33 B // relaxation therapy
34 C // its response to injury often results in more damage
35 A // for a maximum of two days
36 B // worsens existing back pain
37 B // Recommended in certain circumstances
38 A // Strongly recommended
39 B // Recommended in certain circumstances
40 C // Not recommended

If you score ...

0–17	18–27	28–40
you are highly unlikely to get an acceptable score under examination conditions and we recommend that you spend a lot of time improving your English before you take IELTS.	you may get an acceptable score under examination conditions but we recommend that you think about having more practice or lessons before you take IELTS.	you are likely to get an acceptable score under examination conditions but remember that different institutions will find different scores acceptable.

ACADEMIC READING

Each question correctly answered scores 1 mark. Please note! **CORRECT SPELLING NEEDED IN ALL ANSWERS.**

Reading Passage 1, Questions 1–14

1   iv // Undeveloped for centuries
2   i // How the reaction principle works
3   v // The first rockets
4   vii // Rockets for military use
5   B // space travel became a reality
6   D // from the late nineteenth century to the present day
7   A // the Chinese
8   A // the Chinese
9   B // the Indians
10 E // the Americans
11 B
12 E
13 F
14 G

Reading Passage 2, Questions 15–28

15 B // are strongly linked to cigarette smoking
16 A // inhibits the flow of oxygen to the heart
17 C // formation of blood clots
18 NO // N
19 NOT GIVEN // NG
20 YES // Y
21 NOT GIVEN // NG
22 E // is more harmful to non-smokers than to smokers

23 G // is more likely to be at risk of contracting various cancers
24 H // opposes smoking and publishes research on the subject
25 A // a finding of the UCSF study
26 B // an opinion of the UCSF study
27 B // an opinion of the UCSF study
28 C // a finding of the EPA report

Reading Passage 3, Questions 29–40

29 iv // Explaining the inductive method
30 vii // The role of hypotheses in scientific research
31 iii // The testing of hypotheses
32 v // Anticipating results before data is collected
33 vi // How research is done and how it is reported
34 & 35   *IN EITHER ORDER*
    B
    F
36 YES // Y
37 NO // N
38 NOT GIVEN // NG
39 YES // Y
40 D // to help Ph.D students by explaining different conceptions of the research process

If you score ...

0–13	14–25	26–40
you are highly unlikely to get an acceptable score under examination conditions and we recommend that you spend a lot of time improving your English before you take IELTS.	you may get an acceptable score under examination conditions but we recommend that you think about having more practice or lessons before you take IELTS.	you are likely to get an acceptable score under examination conditions but remember that different institutions will find different scores acceptable.

TEST 2

LISTENING

Each question correctly answered scores 1 mark. Please note! **CORRECT SPELLING NEEDED IN ALL ANSWERS.** *(Where alternative spellings are accepted, these are stated in the key.)*

Section 1, Questions 1–10

1   (the) Main Hall
    NOT Hall
2   (the) Director (of) (Studies) // DOS
3   (the) Student(s) Advisor/Adviser
4   eleven/11 o'clock // 11.00 (am)
5   placement/English (test)
6   L // Library
7   MH // Main Hall
8   CL // Computer Laboratory
9   SR // Staff Room
10   SCR // Student Common Room

Section 2, Questions 11–20

11   (overseas)(student(s')) (tuition) fees
12   (the) domestic (area)
13   (essay(s')) deadlines
     NOT essay(s)
14   social (life)
15   outings // trips
16   KOUACHI
17   3269940
18   ten/10(am)–/to 4/four(pm)
19   (an) appointment(s)
20   waiting list

Section 3, Questions 21–30

21   B // staff selection
22   C // disagrees with the rest of the group
23   A // colleagues' ability
24   C // already a part of job interviews
25   selection (procedure)
26–27   *EITHER ORDER*
     (the) (ancient) Chinese
     (the) military // army
28   (almost) two thirds // $\frac{2}{3}$
29   experts
     NOT expert
30   A // describe one selection technique

Section 4, Questions 31–40

31   secondary
32   14 // fourteen (year olds/years old)
33   overlap // overlapping *ACCEPT* over(-)lap // over(-)lapping
34   underside // underneath // bottom
     NOT side
35   on paper // in two dimensions
36   3/three(-)dimensional // 3(-)D
37   *MUST STATE ALL THREE*
     white, grey/gray, brown
38   C
39   D
40   A

If you score ...

0–17	18–27	28–40
you are highly unlikely to get an acceptable score under examination conditions and we recommend that you spend a lot of time improving your English before you take IELTS.	you may get an acceptable score under examination conditions but we recommend that you think about having more practice or lessons before you take IELTS.	you are likely to get an acceptable score under examination conditions but remember that different institutions will find different scores acceptable.

ACADEMIC READING

Each question correctly answered scores 1 mark. Please note! **CORRECT SPELLING NEEDED IN ALL ANSWERS.**

Reading Passage 1, Questions 1–13

1   NOT GIVEN // NG
2   NO // N
3   YES // Y
4   YES // Y
5   NO // N
6   South African
7   French
8   Spanish
9   temperate
10 early spring *NOT* spring
11 2–5 // two to five
12 sub-tropical
13 South African tunneling/tunnelling/ tunneler/tunneller (species)

Reading Passage 2, Questions 14–28

14 v // Governments and management of the environment
15 vii // Farming and food output
16 ii // The environmental impact of modern farming
17 iv // The effects of government policy in rich countries
18 i // The probable effects of the new international trade agreement
19 G // Clearing land for cultivation

20 C // Increased use of chemical inputs
21 F // Soil erosion
22 B // Disappearance of old plant varieties
23 C // was causing significant damage to 20 per cent of farmland
24 B // used twice as much fertiliser as they had in 1960
25 D // farm diversification
26 C // their policies do not recognise the long-term benefit of ending subsidies
27 A // encourage more sustainable farming practices in the long term
28 A // Environmental management

Reading Passage 3, Questions 29–40

29 NOT GIVEN // NG
30 YES // Y
31 YES // Y
32 NOT GIVEN // NG
33 YES // Y
34 NO // N
35 NO // N
36 role sign
37 ritual
38 role sign
39 role set
40 C // a critical study of the importance of role signs in modern society

If you score ...

0–15	16–26	27–40
you are highly unlikely to get an acceptable score under examination conditions and we recommend that you spend a lot of time improving your English before you take IELTS.	you may get an acceptable score under examination conditions but we recommend that you think about having more practice or lessons before you take IELTS.	you are likely to get an acceptable score under examination conditions but remember that different institutions will find different scores acceptable.

TEST 3

LISTENING

Each question correctly answered scores 1 mark. Please note! **CORRECT SPELLING NEEDED IN ALL ANSWERS.** *(Where alternative spellings are accepted these are stated in the key.)*

Section 1, Questions 1–10

1   Rajdoot
2   Park View (Hotel)
3   London Arms
4   208657
5   no/non(-)smoking section/area
6   Lentil curry
7   fifty pound(s)/£50 deposit // deposit (of) £50/fifty pound(s)
8   choose/decide (on)/select (the) menu
9   4 November
    ALTERNATIVE FORMS ACCEPTED
10 (the) Newsletter

Section 2, Questions 11–20

11 (£) 9.50
12 year // annum *NOT* annual
13 reception *NOT* Sports Centre
14 card
15 book
16 weekdays
17 Reception (Area)
18 Dance Studio
19 Squash Courts
20 Fitness Room

Section 3, Questions 21–30

21 Anne Rea
22 (both) 16 (years old)
23 Blind (Jigsaw) Puzzle *NOT* Jigsaw
24 *MUST BE IN ORDER* 20 (cm) 50 (cm) 2.5 (cm) // 2 and a half (cm)
25–27   *IN ANY ORDER*
    safe for children
    (it's) educational
    price (is) good // inexpensive // not expensive // cheap (price) // (is) good price
28 electrics *NOT* electric
29 plastic pieces // in plastic *NOT* pieces
30 1 July
    ALTERNATIVE FORMS ACCEPTED

Section 4, Questions 31–40

31 rabbit (meat)
32 (rather) tough
33 beef
34 (ladies') (feather) fans
35 (delicate) (fine) (good quality) leather
36 meat
37 A // has more protein than beef
38 C // the price of ostrich eggs
39 C // need looking after carefully
40 B // farmed birds are very productive

If you score ...

0–14	15–25	26–40
you are highly unlikely to get an acceptable score under examination conditions and we recommend that you spend a lot of time improving your English before you take IELTS.	you may get an acceptable score under examination conditions but we recommend that you think about having more practice or lessons before you take IELTS.	you are likely to get an acceptable score under examination conditions but remember that different institutions will find different scores acceptable.

ACADEMIC READING

Each question correctly answered scores 1 mark. Please note! **CORRECT SPELLING NEEDED IN ALL ANSWERS.**

Reading Passage 1, Questions 1–12

1 FALSE // F
2 FALSE // F
3 FALSE // F
4 NOT GIVEN // NG
5 TRUE // T
6 TRUE // T
7 TS // Technical Series
8 AT // Artefact Types
9 FA // Field Assemblages
10 AT // Artefact Types
11 FA // Field Assemblages
12 SE // Social Experience

Reading Passage 2, Questions 13–25

13 v // Early research among the Indian Amazons
14 i // Amazonia as unable to sustain complex societies
15 vi // The influence of prehistoric inhabitants on Amazonian natural history
16 NO // N
17 YES // Y
18 NOT GIVEN // NG
19 NO // N
20 YES // Y
21 YES // Y
22 C // were an extremely primitive society
23 A // are evidence of early indigenous communities
24 B // has been shown to be incorrect by recent research
25 C // change present policies on development in the region

Reading Passage 3, Questions 26–40

26 A // They were less able to concentrate
27 B // influences animal feeding habits
28 B // reaction to certain weather phenomena
29 NOT GIVEN // NG
30 FALSE // F
31 FALSE // F
32 TRUE // T
33 TRUE // T
34 NOT GIVEN // NG
35–37 *IN ANY ORDER*
  B // rainy weather
  D // high serotonin levels
  E // sunny weather
38 B // hot weather
39 A // daylight
40 F // time cues

If you score ...

0–14	15–26	27–40
you are highly unlikely to get an acceptable score under examination conditions and we recommend that you spend a lot of time improving your English before you take IELTS.	you may get an acceptable score under examination conditions but we recommend that you think about having more practice or lessons before you take IELTS.	you are likely to get an acceptable score under examination conditions but remember that different institutions will find different scores acceptable.

TEST 4

LISTENING

Each question correctly answered scores 1 mark. Please note! **CORRECT SPELLING NEEDED IN ALL ANSWERS.** *(Where alternative spellings are accepted, these are stated in the key.)*

Section 1, Questions 1–10

1   4.25 // $4\frac{1}{4}$ // four and (a) quarter
2   46 // forty-six
3   A // State Bank
4   D // Library
5   C // Garage
6   (a) (box) (of) chocolates
7   (a) (soft) toy // (a) teddy (bear) // (a) bear
8   (at the) market(s)
9   (at the) market(s)
10 ($)35/thirty-five (dollars)

Section 2, Questions 11–20

11 glass
12 eighteen/18 hours/hrs
13 (a) (strange) taste
14 (the) small size // small // (the) size
15 metal
16 A
17 outside/outdoor activities // outdoors
18 underwater // under/beneath water
19 (a) weak light
20 flashing light

Section 3, Questions 21–30

21 B // hospital
22 C // the middle section

23 C // found it difficult to do
24 C // remove completely
25 B // rewrite
26 C // remove completely
27 Sight and Sound
28 Support Tutor
    NOT Tutor
29 proof reading // proof read
30 10 July
    ALTERNATIVE FORMS ACCEPTED

Section 4, Questions 31–40

31 7.30pm (to/and) 5.30am
    NOT 7.30 to 5.30
32 housewives // housewifes
33 Sunday(s)
34 (about) $25,000/twenty-five thousand dollars
    NOT 25,000
35 C // 67 decibels
36 C // for ceilings
37 W // for walls
38 C // for ceilings
39 D
40 C

If you score ...

0–15	16–26	27–40
you are highly unlikely to get an acceptable score under examination conditions and we recommend that you spend a lot of time improving your English before you take IELTS.	you may get an acceptable score under examination conditions but we recommend that you think about having more practice or lessons before you take IELTS.	you are likely to get an acceptable score under examination conditions but remember that different institutions will find different scores acceptable.

ACADEMIC READING

Each question correctly answered scores 1 mark. Please note! **CORRECT SPELLING NEEDED IN ALL ANSWERS.**

Reading Passage 1, Questions 1–13

1   Los Angeles
2   London
3   Singapore
4   London
5   Los Angeles
6   YES // Y
7   YES // Y
8   NO // N
9   NO // N
10   NO // N
11   A // one
12   D // particulate matter
13   C // the old and ill

Reading Passage 2, Questions 14–27

14   C // the success of the movement's corporate image
15   D // It had a clear purpose and direction
16   **BOTH FOR ONE MARK**
     D // 1918 *AND* E // 1928
17   (selling) advertising (space)
18   colour scheme // (three) colours // purple, white, (and) green
19   (the) Woman's Exhibition
20   NO // N

21   YES // Y
22   NO // N
23   NO // N
24   NOT GIVEN // NG
25   YES // Y
26   YES // Y
27   D // informative

Reading Passage 3, Questions 28–40

28   A // establish whether increased productivity should be sought at any cost
29   C // had identical patterns of organisation
30   C // the staff involved spent a number of months preparing for the study
31   supervision // leadership // management
32   productivity
33   reduced // cut // decreased
34   (group methods of) leadership
35   overstaffed
36   reduced // cut // decreased
37   C // Changes in productivity
38   D // Employees' feelings of responsibility towards completion of work
39   G // Employees feel closer to their supervisors
40   F // Employees' opinion as to extent of personal support from management

If you score ...

0–15	16–27	28–40
you are highly unlikely to get an acceptable score under examination conditions and we recommend that you spend a lot of time improving your English before you take IELTS.	you may get an acceptable score under examination conditions but we recommend that you think about having more practice or lessons before you take IELTS.	you are likely to get an acceptable score under examination conditions but remember that different institutions will find different scores acceptable.

GENERAL TRAINING TEST A

READING

Each question correctly answered scores 1 mark. Please note! **CORRECT SPELLING NEEDED IN ALL ANSWERS.**

Section 1, Questions 1–13

1	B
2	E
3	E
4	C
5	D
6	B
7	***BOTH REQUIRED FOR ONE MARK, IN EITHER ORDER*** A (and) B
8	***BOTH REQUIRED FOR ONE MARK, IN EITHER ORDER*** B (and) D
9	FALSE // F
10	TRUE // T
11	FALSE // F
12	NOT GIVEN // NG
13	TRUE // T

Section 2, Questions 14–26

14	TRUE // T
15	FALSE // F
16	TRUE // T
17	TRUE // T
18	NOT GIVEN // NG
19	FALSE // F

20	(University) Halls of Residence
21	4/four weeks/wks
22	10 to/–15 // ten to fifteen
23	(Waikato) Students' Union
24	(Waikato) river
25	picturesque
26	(ongoing) travel (arrangements)

Section 3, Questions 27–40

27	C // The coal industry and the environment
28	v // Coal as an energy source
29	vi // Coal and the enhanced greenhouse effect
30	vii // Research and development
31	iv // Environment protection measures
32	D // trends in population and lifestyle
33	B // 18 per cent/18%
34	B // developing new gasification techniques
35	A // more cleanly and more efficiently
36	D // runoff water containing sediments
37	NO // N
38	YES // Y
39	YES // Y
40	NOT GIVEN // NG

If you score ...

0–13	14–30	31–40
you are highly unlikely to get an acceptable score under examination conditions and we recommend that you spend a lot of time improving your English before you take IELTS.	you may get an acceptable score under examination conditions but we recommend that you think about having more practice or lessons before you take IELTS.	you are likely to get an acceptable score under examination conditions but remember that different institutions will find different scores acceptable.

GENERAL TRAINING TEST B

READING

Each question correctly answered scores 1 mark. Please note! **CORRECT SPELLING NEEDED IN ALL ANSWERS.**

Section 1, Questions 1–13

1 NO // N
2 YES // Y
3 NO // N
4 NO // N
5 (on the) bottom (of jar)
6 $5 // five dollars
7 (company's) retailing manager
8 place of purchase
9 $50,000
10 ii // Save money by not paying interest
11 i // Payment options
12 vi // Applying for a card
13 v // Location of stores

Section 2, Questions 14–27

14 iii // Film Appreciation Society
15 ix // United Nations Student Club
16 viii // Debating Club
17 iv // Drama Society
18 leave (a) message
19 annually // once a year // every year // each year

20 NO // N
21 YES // Y
22 NOT GIVEN // NG
23 NO // N
24 YES // Y
25 NO // N
26 NO // N
27 YES // Y

Section 3, Questions 28–40

28 F
29 A
30 G
31 E
32 B
33 C
34 NOT GIVEN // NG
35 YES // Y
36 YES // Y
37 YES // Y
38 NO // N
39 NOT GIVEN // NG
40 NO // N

If you score ...

0–15	16–30	31–40
you are highly unlikely to get an acceptable score under examination conditions and we recommend that you spend a lot of time improving your English before you take IELTS.	you may get an acceptable score under examination conditions but we recommend that you think about having more practice or lessons before you take IELTS.	you are likely to get an acceptable score under examination conditions but remember that different institutions will find different scores acceptable.

Model and sample answers for writing tasks

TEST 1, WRITING TASK 1

SAMPLE ANSWER

This is an answer written by a candidate who achieved a Band 5 score. Here is the examiner's comment:

> The writer does what is required of her in terms of task fulfilment, and the message can be followed, but the weaknesses in grammatical control and in spelling cause difficulty for the reader. Complex sentence structures are attempted, but the greatest levels of accuracy are found in basic, simple structures.

This chart shows us that Japanese tourists go abroad for travelling in a decade and Australian's share of marketing for Japanese tourists. Between 1985 and 1995 Japanese tourists travelling abroad was dramatically increased. In 85 there was about 5 milions traveller go abroad. Since 85 number of traveller went up dramatically until 90. It was alomost twice then between 90 and 93 the number rimain stateable, which is about 12 millions. From 93 to 95 it rose slightly. Therefore in 1995 there were about 15 millions people went abroad.

I am going to write about the other chart, which is Australian's share of Japanese's tourist market. This is also between 1985 and 1995. About 2 million Japanese tourist went to Australia in 1985. Between 85 and 89 people went there is increased sharply, which is almost 3 times more. In 1990 it fall number slightly but from 90 to 94 number is went up. However 94 to 95 is not so went up number of people who went to Australia. It rimain is the same or slightly decreased.

TEST 1, WRITING TASK 2

SAMPLE ANSWER

This is an answer written by a candidate who achieved a Band 4 score. Here is the examiner's comment:

> The majority of this answer has no relation to the task set: the first half is completely irrelevant and the second part is only marginally related to the topic. The candidate has therefore been penalised for this. There is little meaningful message, and grammatical control is weak.

I DISAGREE

Nowadays, football is the most popular game in the world. We can find there are many different teams who plays this football. There are dividing into 3 division: division one, division two and division three. Each divisions have different skills. The skills that they have are depend on the manager. He is the one who teachs the player how to play. By playing football, there are many advantages and disadvantages. Firstly, the team can earn a lot of money. If we compare the income in division one and division two are really different. The division one will get more than division two. Because as we know, the team in division one, they shows to the people that they are able to play better than the others. For example: David Beckham (the player of Manchaster United). He can earn for about £45.000 £50.000/week. It's unbelievable. Even the prime minister in the UK just got for about £110.000/year. Secondly, they can get a lot of spectators which makes the income increased. In one match, they can earn for about 20 or 30 million pounds. Actually, it's really high. For one ticket (VIP) it can cost us a lot of money. I think for about £100 or over. That is for one person. How if we count for a million person? There are also many disadvantages: like from the task which says that the releasing patriotic emotions in a safe way. Actually, I don't really agree about that: like 2 weeks or 3 weeks ago, there are 2 fans of Leeds United got shots. And it makes them died. Many people come and give them flowers and also the clothes which shown they're sad about that.

There are other sport games like tennis. Tennis is also popular. In playing tennis there are also have advantages and disadvantages. This games shows how they against each other. The advantages are can earn a lot of money, can attract the spectators (audience). There are also have disadvantages of this games. For example: two years ago, when Monica Sales and Steffi Graph are on the match. They play against each other then, one of the Steffi's fan can't stand anymore, he killed (shots) Monica Sales. That makes Monica Sales have to stop the game. The people are all thinking to take her to the hospital. Because of that, it makes Monica Sales stopped from playing tennis for about a year. But now, she has started again.

In my opinion, these sport can ease the international tensions and also can make death from year to year become increase. So, it is very dangerous.

TEST 2, WRITING TASK 1

MODEL ANSWER

This model has been prepared by an examiner as an example of a very good answer. However, please note that this is just one example out of many possible approaches.

The chart shows that Britain, among the four European countries listed, has spent most heavily on the range of consumer goods included. In every case, British spending is considerably higher than that of other countries; only in the case of tennis racquets does another country, Italy, come close.

In contrast, Germany is generally the lowest spender. This is most evident in photographic film, where Germany spends much less than Britain. Germany only spends more than another country, France, in two cases: tennis racquets and perfumes.

Meanwhile, France and Italy generally maintain middle positions, averaging approximately similar spending overall. Specifically, France spends more on CDs and photographic film but less on tennis racquets than Italy does. Italy's spending on personal stereos is only marginally greater than that of France, while spending on toys is equal between the two.

It is clear from the data given that there are some significant differences in spending habits within Europe.

TEST 2, WRITING TASK 2

MODEL ANSWER

This model has been prepared by an examiner as an example of a very good answer. However, please note that this is just one example out of many possible approaches.

Overall, I disagree with the opinion expressed. I would like to begin by pointing out that 'traditional skills and ways of life' are not automatically of one country, but of a culture or community.

In many ways, the history of civilisation is the history of technology: from the discovery of fire to the invention of the wheel to the development of the Internet, we have been moving on from previous ways of doing things. Some technologies, such as weapons of mass destruction, are of negative impact. Others, such as medical advances, positively help people to live better or longer, and so very much help traditional ways of life. Surely, few people would seek to preserve such traditions as living in caves!

Interestingly, technology can positively contribute to the keeping alive of traditional skills and ways of life. For example, the populations of some islands are too small to have normal schools. Rather than breaking up families by sending children to the mainland, education authorities have been able to use the Internet to deliver schooling online. In addition, the Internet, and modern refrigeration techniques, are being used to keep alive the traditional skills of producing salmon; it can now be ordered from, and delivered to, anywhere in the world.

In conclusion, without suggesting that *all* technology is necessarily good, I think it is by no means 'pointless', in any way, to try to keep traditions alive with technology. We should not ignore technology, because it can be our friend and support our way of life.

TEST 3, WRITING TASK 1

MODEL ANSWER

This model has been prepared by an examiner as an example of a very good answer. However, please note that this is just one example out of many possible approaches.

The data shows the differences between developing and industrialised countries' participation in education and science.

In terms of the number of years of schooling received, we see that the length of time people spend at school in industrialised countries was much greater at 8.5 years in 1980, compared to 2.5 years in developing countries. The gap was increased further in 1990 when the figures rose to 10.5 years and 3.5 years respectively.

We can see a similar pattern in the second graph, which shows that the number of people working as scientists and technicians in industrialised countries increased from 55 to 85 per 1,000 people between 1980 and 1990, while the number in developing countries went from 12 to 20.

Finally, the figures for spending on research and development show that industrialised countries more than doubled their spending, from $200bn to $420bn, whereas developing countries actually decreased theirs, from $75bn down to $25bn.

Overall we can see that not only are there very large differences between the two economies but that these gaps are widening.

TEST 3, WRITING TASK 2

MODEL ANSWER

This model has been prepared by an examiner as an example of a very good answer. However, please note that this is just one example out of many possible approaches.

> The issue of children doing paid work is a complex and sensitive one. It is difficult to say who has the right to judge whether children working is 'wrong' or 'valuable'. Opinions will also differ as to 'learning' benefits: no doubt teachers and factory owners, for example, would have varying concerns.
>
> An important consideration is the kind of work undertaken. Young children doing arduous and repetitive tasks on a factory production line, for example, are less likely to be 'learning' than older children helping in an old people's home. There are health and safety issues to be considered as well. It is an unfortunate fact that many employers may prefer to use the services of children simply to save money by paying them less than adults and it is this type of exploitation that should be discouraged.
>
> However, in many countries children work because their families need the additional income, no matter how small. This was certainly the case in the past in many industrialized countries, and it is very difficult to judge that it is wrong for children today to contribute to the family income in this way.
>
> Nevertheless, in better economic circumstances, few parents would choose to send their children out to full-time paid work. If learning responsibilities and work experience are considered to be important, then children can acquire these by having light, part-time jobs or even doing tasks such as helping their parents around the family home, which are unpaid, but undoubtedly of value in children's development.

TEST 4, WRITING TASK 1

SAMPLE ANSWER

This is an answer written by a candidate who achieved a Band 7 score. Here is the examiner's comment:

> This is a good account of the information presented in the graph, although occasionally the organisation of the data is slightly unusual. The writer grasps all the key points, however, and supports these with figures, before providing a summary of the main points. Sentence structures are more than adequate, although the writer has some problems with the use of tenses and prepositions. There are minor examples of unsuitable register (e.g. 'turned out', 'disastrous', and one contracted verb form), but as there are only a few instances of this, the candidate has not been penalised.

According to the results of the labour-force research published recently, the following conclusions can be drawn from it:

In March, 1993, United States had seven percent of their workforce which might not seem disastrous until compared with Japan, where 2.5% were unemployed. However, the unemployment rate in United States began declining slowly since March 1993, and reached 5% mark in the middle of 1996. Japan turned out to be less lucky, as their unemployment rate doubled in three years. From then on, the percentage of unemployed workforce in United States remained roughly the same – about 5% until March 99, although there were minor falls and rises in the unemployment rate.

As for Japan, the percentage of unemployed fell rapidly by 0.5–0.6% after March 1996, but from summer 1996 and onwards it grew steadily and without any falls to reach 5.0% boundary in March 1999.

The major conclusion that I've drawn using the graph, is that number of unemployed in USA decreased by about 2.0% in the course of six years, while in Japan it actually increased by 2.5% percent. As a result, in March 99, both Japan and US had about 5% of their work force unemployed.

TEST 4, WRITING TASK 2

SAMPLE ANSWER

This is an answer written by a candidate who achieved a Band 6 score. Here is the examiner's comment:

> The writer expresses a point of view, but the ideas show little development and the argument does not go anywhere. The writing is well-organised, however, and can be followed with little difficulty. Sentence structures are sufficiently varied, but grammatical and lexical control is quite often faulty (e.g. subject/verb agreement, incorrect use of tenses, mass/count nouns).

In balancing the world economic growth, the underdevelopment of the Third World Nations have been drawn to the attention of the developed countries of the Western. Thus, governmental policies and interference in the agricultural business of the poorer nations were made to secure their dominant source of the economy. Many discussions among economists and politicians also put their focus on the other aspects. That is, to improve the health, education and trade for the developing countries. However, the improvements cannot be made by these countries, but more external assistance and aids should be done.

Because of the shortage of food supply, the people in poorer nations (i.e. Africa) are esily prone to disease, hunger and death. When natural or environmental disastres happen, they are threaten with their lives. Education cannot be well developed as a result of frequent droughts, famines and disease spreading. The other countries, while emphasising on the development of agriculture in the Third World, cannot really give the solution to the cyclical problem which has been existing for a long time. It is time to consider the consequences of all the waste of efforts in trying to help the economic growth of the Third World and to think from the other perspectives. The richer countries have the power to rebuilt the Third World by taking care the essentials – health, education and trade. More aids for providing the medicine, educational needs and materials can be done by the richer countries. The assistance of trade and developing business in the poorer countries also can be of a great help to the poorer nations.

If the richer countries can be more serious about the essential issues of how a nation develops, and well consider the special situations and circumstances those poorer nations are facing, the improvements will be more efficiently made. The governments of developed countries are, in some ways, responsible – though not obliged – for the future of those developing countries.

TEST A, WRITING TASK 1 (GENERAL TRAINING)

MODEL ANSWER

This model has been prepared by an examiner as an example of a very good answer. However, please note that this is just one example out of many possible approaches.

Dear Ms Barnes,

I am writing concerning the position of Assistant Office Manager that I am due to begin next Monday. However, a problem has arisen.

As you know, I currently work for my uncle's food-packing business, and you will remember from my interview that I have gained valuable experience there. Unfortunately, he has had to go into hospital for an operation, leaving my aunt in charge of both the home and the business. She has asked me, as this is a particularly busy time of year, to stay on and help her with the running of the office.

I realise this will be inconvenient to you, but very much hope that, given the circumstances, you would be prepared to allow me to take up my position with you two weeks later than planned.

I would like to emphasise that I remain very keen to work with you, and that I will be gaining further useful experience during this time.

I look forward to hearing from you.

Yours sincerely,

John Forbes

TEST A, WRITING TASK 2 (GENERAL TRAINING)

MODEL ANSWER

This model has been prepared by an examiner as an example of a very good answer. However, please note that this is just one example out of many possible approaches.

Today, education has become a priority for many parents seeking to secure a good future for their children in this rapidly changing world. They believe that if their children apply themselves and work hard at school, then they will increase their opportunities for going to higher education and eventually getting a good job. Of course they are right, and as access to the best education and best jobs is becoming more competitive, then it is true that children have to make the best of their study time when they are young.

However, the parents who do not allow their children sufficient free time for leisure activities outside school hours, are misguided. Such activities are far from being a waste of time for the children simply because they are not academic. It is important to remember that children need to develop skills other than intellectual ones, and the best way to do this is through activities such as sports, games and playing with other kids. If they cannot play make-believe games, how can they develop their imagination? How can they learn physical co-ordination or learn important social lessons about winning and losing if they do not practise any sports? Many children form strong, personal relationships with the friends they play with, and without the opportunity to do this, they could grow up emotionally immature or unformed.

Finally, I think it is also important to remember that children need to relax as well as work. If everything they do must have some educational or academic relevance, then they will soon get tired of studying altogether, which is the last thing parents would want.

TEST B, WRITING TASK 1 (GENERAL TRAINING)

SAMPLE ANSWER

This is an answer written by a candidate who achieved a Band 7 score. Here is the examiner's comment:

> The response to the task is fluent, although there is room for expansion and clarification of some aspects of the task. The message is well-organised and can be followed throughout, with the writer making good use of 'signpost' words. There are some problems with word choice and with word formation (e.g. 'big noise', 'distractive'), but the range of sentence structures is varied and well-controlled for accuracy.

Dear Sir/Madam,

I am writing with regard to the article in your newspaper dated 7th September. My house is situated within 20 minutes walk of the airport. Please allow me to point out the problems which have caused serious damage on the residential area. I am fully sure that the problems must be aggravated if the plan is carried out to expand the airport and increase the number of flights.

First of all, the low-flying aeroplanes are utterly distractive. They make such a big noise that I cannot concentrate on housework at all. What is worse, I am woken up by the late hour flights at midnight; I was diagnosed as insomnia the other day. I should call this situation noise pollution.

Secondly, I am afraid that the expansion of the airport may reduce the plot of land for the playground which is under construction near the airport at the moment.

To sum up, I strongly disagree with the plan. I would appreciate if you could possibly write the article about the problems and disagreement as I said above.

Yours faithfully,

TEST B, WRITING TASK 2 (GENERAL TRAINING)

SAMPLE ANSWER

This is an answer written by a candidate who achieved a Band 6 score. Here is the examiner's comment:

> The answer is an adequate response to the task, although there are not many ideas and there is little development of these. The response reads fairly easily, however, and the writer's intention is usually clear. There is a variety of sentence structures, and although these are not always grammatically accurate, the errors do not interfere with the message. There are signs of vocabulary limitations.

The today's family-life changed a lot. Many parents are divorce, a lot of mothers and fathers have their job's far away from home. The children are often alone and lonley . . . but what are the reasons for this happening?

First of all, I think that the modern technology is one of the main reason for this problem. Many parents work in their nearest cities from their home. They work with computer in big offices and came home late at night. However, they have no time to look after their children.

In the past, families used to work "as a family". Every member worked hard and helped the family to survife, for example farmers. Furthermore, the education used to be controled by the parents, not like today's day-schools with teachers and professors. On the other hand, there must be a solution to bring separeted families together. At my point of view, families should spend their free time together. I am thinking about weekends or the time after work. Children need their parents even when they are older. To give a reasonable example: I often go out with my parents, mostly for a dinner. Then my brother and I speak about our future plans or something else. An intensiv conversation is a possible solution. A similar way is, to divide your job into half-part work-times and spend your free time leftover with your loved persons. A point against this statement is to have financial problems.

To sum up I wish that every family is as close as possible with each other, if they like that.

Sample answer sheets

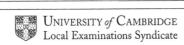

PENCIL must be used to complete sheet.

Centre number:

Please write your **name** below,

0 1 2 3 4 5 6 7 8 9
0 1 2 3 4 5 6 7 8 9
0 1 2 3 4 5 6 7 8 9
0 1 2 3 4 5 6 7 8 9

X

then write your four digit Candidate number in the boxes and
shade the number in the grid on the right in PENCIL.

Test date (shade ONE box for the day, ONE box for the month and ONE box for the year):

Day: 1 2 3 4 5 6 7 8 9 10 11 12 13 14 15 16 17 18 19 20 21 22 23 24 25 26 27 28 29 30 31

Month: 1 2 3 4 5 6 7 8 9 10 11 12   Last digit of the **Year:** 0 1 2 3 4 5 6 7 8 9

IELTS Listening Answer Sheet

Version number:
Please enter the number in the boxes and shade the number in the grid.

0 1 2 3 4 5 6 7 8 9
0 1 2 3 4 5 6 7 8 9

#		✓ X
1		1
2		2
3		3
4		4
5		5
6		6
7		7
8		8
9		9
10		10
11		11
12		12
13		13
14		14
15		15
16		16
17		17
18		18
19		19
20		20
21		21

#		✓ X
22		22
23		23
24		24
25		25
26		26
27		27
28		28
29		29
30		30
31		31
32		32
33		33
34		34
35		35
36		36
37		37
38		38
39		39
40		40

Band Score		Listening Total	

Marker's initials	

171

IELTS Reading Answer Sheet

Module taken (shade one box below):

Academic ⬜   General Training ⬜

Version number:
Please enter the number
in the boxes and shade
the number in the grid.

0 1 2 3 4 5 6 7 8 9
0 1 2 3 4 5 6 7 8 9

#		✓ / X
1		✓ 1 X
2		2
3		3
4		4
5		5
6		6
7		7
8		8
9		9
10		10
11		11
12		12
13		13
14		14
15		15
16		16
17		17
18		18
19		19
20		20
21		21
22		22
23		23
24		24
25		25
26		26
27		27
28		28
29		29
30		30

#		✓ / X
31		✓ 31 X
32		32
33		33
34		34
35		35
36		36
37		37
38		38
39		39
40		40

Band Score		Listening Total	

Marker's initials	